Day by Day with God

September–December 2004

The Editor writes...

What is God like? Where do we fit into his action plans? How do we cope when life's outlook seems bleak and we are losing sight of the big picture? During the next four months we will be looking into the Bible to find some answers.

But first, take the opportunity to make a fresh start. The education system has drilled many of us into thinking the year starts in September. Anne Coomes takes up this theme to look at new beginnings throughout Scripture. Hilary McDowell then takes up her pen to ask who we are following as we step forward into the future. Can we accept Jesus as Lord as well as friend and comforter?

Our God is more multi-faceted than the most intricately cut diamond. From one perspective he is Lord and King of all creation, as Hilary and Diana Archer both show; but the prophet Hosea saw him as the deserted husband, betrayed by a wayward wife. At the end of September, with Kristina Petersen's help, discover how our rebelliousness breaks God's heart, then delight in the fact that still he longs to draw us back into his intimate embrace.

God's love can be tough and his treatment does not always seem tender. Life's hard places are often part of his shaping process. Sometimes there is no apparent reason for the way life turns out, as Job discovered. Jennifer Rees Larcombe shows us how Job coped with tremendous loss but could still say, 'How my heart yearns within me!' when he looked forward to seeing God face to face. Nothing Satan could throw at him could destroy Job's longing for God. That's faith! And Job didn't even know about Jesus! Now God's plan for humanity has been revealed in his Son. We are mysteriously united with him and with all believers, as Christina Rees highlights in her notes.

Jesus, the one whose birth we celebrate in this season, is the focus of all history. Hebrews sums up the story, as Christine Platt reveals. His life, death and resurrection make sense when we see them as part of God's rescue plan for humanity. It's a theme we will return to in more depth during next year. In this series of notes, let it prompt an Advent full of praise and wonder at what God has done for us in Christ. Molly Dow sets the tone with her notes on praise taken from the Psalms. Bridget Plass adds the sparkle and mystery of a short series on angels, then Chris Leonard rounds off the year with

Contents

The Bible Reading Fellowship,
First Floor, Elsfield Hall, 15–17 Elsfield Way, Oxford OX2 8FG
E-mail: enquiries@brf.org.uk

First published in Great Britain 2004

ISBN 1 84101 313 7

Jacket design: JAC Design for Print, Crowborough

Trade representation in UK:
Lion Publishing plc, Mayfield House, 256 Banbury Road
Oxford OX2 7DH

Distributed in Australia by:
Willow Connection, PO Box 288, Brookvale, NSW 2100.
Tel: 02 9948 3957; Fax: 02 9948 8153;
E-mail: info@willowconnection.com.au

Distributed in New Zealand by:
Scripture Union Wholesale, PO Box 760, Wellington
Tel: 04 385 0421; Fax: 04 384 3990; E-mail: suwholesale@clear.net.nz

Distributed in South Africa by:
Struik Christian Books, PO Box 1144, Capetown 8000
Tel: 021 462 4630; Fax: 021 461 3612; E-mail: enquiry@struik.co.za

Acknowledgments
Scriptures from The New Revised Standard Version of the Bible, Anglicized Edition, copyright © 1989, 1995 by the Division of Christian Education of the National Council of the Churches of Christ in the USA, used by permission. All rights reserved.

Scriptures from The Revised Standard Version of the Bible, copyright © 1946, 1952, 1971 by the Division of Christian Education of the National Council of the Churches of Christ in the USA, used by permission. All rights reserved.

New King James Version of the Bible copyright © 1979, 1980, 1982 by Thomas Nelson, Inc. All rights reserved.

Scripture quotations taken from *The Holy Bible, New International Version*, copyright © 1973, 1978, 1984 by International Bible Society. Used by permission of Hodder & Stoughton Ltd. All rights reserved. 'NIV' is a registered trademark of International Bible Society. UK trademark number 1448790.

Scriptures quoted from the Good News Bible published by The Bible Societies/HarperCollins Publishers, copyright © 1966, 1971, 1976, 1992, American Bible Society.

Scriptures quoted from the *Contemporary English Version* published by The Bible Societies/HarperCollins Publishers, copyright © 1991, 1992, 1995 American Bible Society.

Scripture quotations from THE MESSAGE. Copyright © by Eugene H. Peterson 1993, 1994, 1995. Used by permission of NavPress Publishing.

Printed in Great Britain by Bookmarque, Croydon

DAY BY DAY WITH GOD

Bible Readings for Women

SEPTEMBER–DECEMBER 2004

Christina Press
BRF
Tunbridge Wells/Oxford

a party note. Those who find festive partying painful will find a kindred spirit in Chris—but should also find deeper reasons to make this Christmas a season for celebration.

Like diamonds, we are all different. Let God's word hone you into shape as you use these notes, and let his light shine through you to a world that needs to know what God is like and where we all fit into his plans for human history.

New for 2005

Who was it who said 'Men are like a chest-of-drawers and women are like wardrobes—you open the doors and everything falls out!' I assume they meant that men often like to tackle one subject at a time and women like the big picture, even if that might seem to be the messy option.

The gender stereotypes might not be accurate, but each of us has different ways of working. Thinking about the different ways in which we approach life turned me to thinking about how we tackle the Bible. So often we pull out the 'Psalms drawer' to study that particular book; or we pull out the 'themes drawer' and trace some of the Bible themes, like 'new beginnings' and 'parties' in this issue.

What would it be like to adopt a 'wardrobe' mentality to look at the Bible? Is it possible to see the big picture? As I've tried to look at the Bible for the big picture, I've been thrilled to see how God has worked through the whole of history, from the dawn of time to the present day, with the promise of a future with him. God has rescued us from sin and death and has planned an eternity in his love for those who believe.

In 2005, along with a fresh new cover design, *Day by Day with God* will be tracing God's rescue plan through the Bible. For those readers who like the notes as they are, we will still be looking at themes, characters and Bible books. But for those who like to look at the big picture, those themes will weave together through the year as we grasp the big picture of God's rescue plan for people like us.

Catherine Butcher

Contributors

Diana Archer is a writer and editor, and has three teenage children. Starting a church in her lounge with her husband Graham, an Anglican vicar, led to her writing *Who'd Plant a Church?* (Christina Press), a warts-and-all account of church and vicarage life. She now works with the Damaris Trust in Southampton, producing Connect Bible studies, a popular group resource linking the word to the world online and in print.

Anne Coomes has been a journalist for the Church of England for over 25 years. She and the Revd Taffy Davies, a well-known vicar/artist, own and run www.Parishpump.co.uk, a resource website for church magazine editors. Anne is working on her Masters degree in Mission Studies. She is Editor of *Decision Magazine UK*, the magazine for the Billy Graham Association and Samaritan's Purse. She is also Reader for her parish in north Cheshire.

Molly Dow is the Spirituality Adviser for Carlisle Diocese. She is married to Graham, the Bishop of Carlisle, and they have four adult children and three grandchildren. She has produced and taught courses on prayer and other aspects of spiritual life and growth and written *Mountains and Molehills*. She has a degree in chemistry and a diploma in theology, and is a Reader.

Jennifer Rees Larcombe, one of Britain's best-loved Christian authors and speakers, lives in Kent. She writes from a recent experience of walking in the shadows. She contributes regularly to Christian magazines, including a problem page, and has recently published a book on the ministry of angels, a children's Bible story book and an account of her dramatic recovery, *Unexpected Healing*.

Chris Leonard has two 20-something 'children' and lives with her husband in Surrey. She has a degree in English and theology and her thirteen books range from biography and devotional to children's stories. She enjoys leading creative writing workshops and holidays because 'people are so interesting—and they grow!' Recent BRF publications include *The Heart of Christmas*.

Hilary McDowell is a deaconess in Belfast, now living by faith, with a ministry of reconciliation, prayer healing and outreach through poetry, art, drama and music. Her books, *Some Day I'm Going to Fly* (with foreword by Adrian Plass) and *Around the World in 80 Prayers*, have made her name known internationally. She has also written *On the Way to Bethlehem* (a book for Advent) and *Visit to a Second Favourite Planet*, both published by BRF.

Kristina Petersen works for BRF and as a freelance writer. She writes for a number of Christian magazines and newspapers. She started writing while she was a member of the Lee Abbey community, where she edited and wrote for their quarterly magazine *Rapport*. Kristina lives in Oxford and is single.

Bridget Plass has a gift for seeing Jesus in the ordinary messiness of real life. She has recently written a Lent book for BRF, *Challenges of the Narrow Way*, and leads occasional Quiet Days for BRF. As well as writing and speaking herself, she arranges her husband Adrian's diary and, when family commitments allow, she accompanies him on tour.

Christine Platt worked for ten years with The Navigators, living in Ivory Coast and ravelling widely throughout Africa. She has written booklets, articles and the SU *Lifebuilder* study book on 'Forgiveness'. She now lives in New Zealand.

Christina Rees is a well-known writer and broadcaster, contributing to BBC Radio 4's *Thought for the Day* and many other radio and television programmes. She speaks and preaches widely and is a professional life and business coach. Christina is also a member of the General Synod of the Church of England and Chair of WATCH (Women and the Church), a national organization that promotes the ministries of women in the church. Her books include *The Divine Embrace* and *Voices of this Calling*.

Contributors are identified by their initials at the bottom of each page.

A Morning Prayer

Thank you, heavenly Father,
for this new day.
Be with me now
in all I do
and think
and say,
that it will be to your glory.

Amen

All change for autumn

You will be a blessing. I will bless those who bless you.

The August Bank Holiday is over. So, more or less, is summer. It's 'all change' time. Soon the schools will go back. Our diaries are filling up with a new round of commitments. After the drowsiness of August, the tempo of life is quickening again. We all face new beginnings of one sort or another this month.

For many of us, these new beginnings are eagerly awaited. New schools, university, getting back to work or even starting retirement all bring us greater scope. New beginnings in our private lives can also mean great joy: a new relationship, marriage, a new baby, new home.

Perhaps, though, the new beginning ahead of you this autumn is not so welcome. You may be picking up the pieces of your life after failed exams or redundancy, financial problems. You may be climbing out of the ruins of a marriage or struggling with increasing illness or deep mourning after bereavement.

To get the most out of whatever lies ahead for you this month, it is worth pausing to consider what the Bible has to say about new beginnings. The very first verse of Genesis opens with 'In the beginning…' That was the first beginning ever, if you like—when God created a perfect earth. This first beginning lasts precisely the first two chapters of Genesis, for in chapter 3 Adam and Eve rebel against God.

However, the story does not end there—God makes another new beginning. From Genesis chapter 4 onwards, the Bible is full of new beginnings of every conceivable kind. In fact, God's rescue plan for the whole human race begins with his calling one man to make a new beginning. His name is Abraham. His willingness to respond to God about 4000 years ago went on to shape world history.

Father, help me to respond willingly to you, whatever this month has in store, and let me be a blessing to others, helping to influence their lives for good, too.

AC

First, make a good ending

There is a time for everything, and a season for every activity under heaven.

To begin *before* the beginning, 'In my *end* is my beginning.' So observed T.S. Eliot (1888–1965) in his famous poem 'East Coker'—the second of his *Four Quartets* (the italics are mine.)

Every new beginning in our lives means an end of something else—that which went before. How well we complete that ending will affect how well we can go on to make the next new beginning.

We teach children to tidy up one mess before they begin another and perhaps we should heed that advice in our adult lives! There is a fashionable word for it: 'closure'. It means taking stock of what has happened to us, reaching acceptance of it, then, finally, letting go, so that our way is cleared for a new beginning.

Of course, endings happen to us in different ways. Some are voluntary, when we are happy to move on to something new. Some are voluntary, but reluctantly made—you have loved what you have had. Other endings are involuntary—when the plug is simply pulled on you, either by impersonal events or a particular person. These endings can be shattering.

Whatever your new beginning may be this autumn, take time to prayerfully ponder Ecclesiastes 3:1–14. It is full of endings and beginnings and reassures us that God 'has made everything beautiful in its time'. Remember, too, 'When my spirit grows faint within me, it is you who know my way…' (Psalm 142:3). God does not make mistakes. He says, 'I make known the end from the beginning… My purpose will stand, and I will do all that I please' (Isaiah 46:10).

Father God, the First and the Last, the Beginning and the End (Revelation 22:13). I am so glad that you know all about my endings as well as my beginnings. Help me to trust you through life's difficulties as well as in happy times. Enable me to have good endings so I can make good beginnings.

AC

Term time

Wisdom will enter your heart, and knowledge will be pleasant to your soul. Discretion will protect you, and understanding will guard you.

'Though it cost all you have, get understanding', says Proverbs 4:7. Perhaps that Old Testament writer foresaw the high cost of modern education!

Of all the new beginnings of autumn, education is the one nearly all of us have experienced. If at present you or a member of your family is packing for college or university, you will be encouraged by what the Bible has to say about learning.

It should come as no surprise that the God who created our fantastically complicated brains wants us to use them. The Bible encourages this constantly. Hence, 'learning' is mentioned 107 times in the Bible; 'knowledge' gets 131 mentions; 'wisdom' is urged 416 times and 'understanding' 272 times.

The Bible praises those who take the trouble and effort to learn: '... you who are foolish, gain understanding' (Proverbs 8:5); 'Wise men store up knowledge' (Proverbs 10:14); 'The discerning heart seeks knowledge' (Proverbs 15:14); and 'The lips of the wise spread knowledge' (Proverbs 15:7).

The Bible is scathing about those who don't want to learn: '... fools hate knowledge' (Proverbs 1:22); '... fools despise wisdom and discipline' (Proverbs 1:7). So where do you begin? Job (34:4) urges '... let us learn together what is good' and Proverbs spells it out: 'The fear of the Lord is the beginning of knowledge' (Proverbs 1:7).

As Christians, we are urged not only to develop and expand our God-given intelligence and talents, but to do so seeing the wider picture: our world and ourselves created and sustained by God. Hence, God's people should also take time to learn about God, 'so that they may learn to revere me' (Deuteronomy 4:10).

Jesus said, 'Take my yoke upon you and learn from me, for I am gentle and humble in heart, and you will find rest for your souls' (Matthew 11:29). Ask Jesus to be your teacher, spiritual director or life coach. Listen carefully to what he teaches you today.

AC

How to get that wall built

Give your servant success today by granting him favour.

If you are beginning a challenging project this autumn, Nehemiah is the book for you. This amazing prophet wrote the manual on how to succeed at work. Following invasion in the fifth century BC, Jerusalem's walls were broken down, the city left defenceless. Nehemiah determined to take action. His methods are startlingly relevant today.

- *He sees that the job needs to be done:* 'Its gates have been burned with fire' (Nehemiah 1:3).
- *He makes sure God wants him to do the job:* 'I mourned and fasted and prayed before the God of heaven' (1:4).
- *He keeps his own counsel and researches the project thoroughly:* 'I set out during the night with a few men. I had not told anyone what my God had put in my heart' (2:12).
- *Nehemiah then calls the local leaders together and motivates them:* 'You see the trouble we are in… Come, let us rebuild' (2:17).
- *He organizes them to begin the work in bite-sized chunks:* Nehemiah 3 lists who did what, where.
- *Nehemiah perseveres, despite criticism and attacks—and takes sensible precautions:* 'We prayed… and posted a guard' (4:9).
- *Nehemiah works hard and long:* 'from the first light of dawn till the stars came out' (4:21).
- *Nehemiah does not misuse his authority:* '… out of reverence for God I did not act like that. Instead, I devoted myself to the work on this wall' (5:15).
- *He refuses to be waylaid by other people's agendas:* 'I am carrying on a great project and cannot go down' (6:3). He stays focused.
- *In due course, Nehemiah is successful:* 'So the wall was completed' (6:15).
- *Finally, Nehemiah makes sure the project will continue to be a success and properly administered:* 'I put in charge of Jerusalem… Hanani, along with Hananiah' (7:2).

Father, help me to keep my focus on you. Whether you choose to use me in small secret ways or in large public projects, may my life make an impact for good on other people.

AC

Homes

But as for me and my household, we will serve the Lord.

Moving house is a major new beginning. The Bible has a lot to say about houses. The Hebrew word for house—*bayit*—occurs over 2000 times. If you are about to move house, consider the following. Proverbs advises you to make sure that you can afford it: 'Finish your outdoor work and get your fields ready; after that, build your house' (24:27).

Homes are things that grow with careful planning and time: 'The wise woman builds her house…' (Proverbs 14:1); 'In the house of the wise are stores of choice food and oil…' (Proverbs 21:20); 'By wisdom a house is built… through knowledge its rooms are filled with rare and beautiful treasures' (Proverbs 24:3).

True homes are built on harmony rather than material possessions: 'Better a dry crust with peace and quiet than a house full of feasting, with strife' (Proverbs 17:1).

You can please God by your generosity. Paul urges the Christians in Rome to 'practise hospitality' (Romans 12:13), and you can use your home for Christian outreach. The early Church met in the homes of people like Priscilla and Aquila (Acts 18:18) and Apphia and Archippus (Philemon 1:2).

Jesus did not have a home: '… the Son of Man has nowhere to lay his head' (Matthew 8:20) and he knew how hard it is to give up a home: '… no one who has left home… for me and the gospel will fail to receive a hundred times as much…' (Mark 10:29, 30).

When Jesus tried to explain eternity, he didn't do so by dazzling us with stories of harps and trumpets and clouds, but of an eternal home: 'In my Father's house are many rooms… I am going there to prepare a place for you…' (John 14:2). That will be our last new home—and the best.

Thank God for your home and why not dedicate each room to the Lord? Have a house blessing and say, along with Joshua, '… as for me and my household, we will serve the Lord' (Joshua 24:15).

AC

Unity through love

Love… always protects, always trusts, always hopes, always perseveres.

If your new beginning this autumn is marriage, you are about to take the most momentous step of your life. Your husband's character, ability and morals will directly affect you from now on. The Bible warns us of this. With apologies to the writer of Proverbs for changing the gender, consider the following: 'A husband of noble character who can find? He is worth far more than rubies. His wife has full confidence in him and lacks nothing of value. He brings her good, not harm, all the days of his life' (31:10–12).

Does this sound like your fiancé? Sadly, 'charm is deceptive, and beauty is fleeting' (31:30). Good character outlasts handsome features.

If your wedding is soon, you'll both be up to your eyes in preparations. Remember, though, that the dress, cake, church, flowers, reception and all the rest are for one day only. There are other more important preparations that need to be made—by both of you. Remember Professor Higgins in My *Fair Lady* when he sings 'why don't they straighten up *the mess that's inside?*'

All of us have a 'mess that's inside'. It's human nature. The Holy Spirit wants to straighten it up for us—he is preparing us to be the bride of Christ one day—but surely what improves us for our 'heavenly bridegroom' will also help when it comes to living with each other here on earth.

Paul writes, '… clothe yourselves with compassion, kindness, humility, gentleness and patience. Bear with each other and forgive whatever grievances you may have against one another. Forgive as the Lord forgave you. And over all these virtues put on love, which binds them all together in perfect unity' (Colossians 3:12–14).

This kind of preparation is much harder, but is vital. The soap operas on TV are full of examples of what happens when all the preparations for marriage are made only on the outside and not in our hearts as well.

Pray for some of the married couples you know. Ask God to bind them together in perfect unity.

AC

When you're betrayed and abandoned

I will take refuge in the shadow of your wings until the disaster has passed.

You started out so well—full of dreams and possibilities for the years ahead. Then you met him. Maybe there were small things that should have warned you, but the relationship developed, full of affection and promise. You loved him. You trusted him... Then, WHAM—deceit, disillusionment, abandonment, loss.

Are you just emerging from a disastrous relationship? Read the story of Samson in Judges 13—16. It will cheer you up. No matter how misplaced your love has been, you cannot have made as big a mistake as Samson did. When it comes to persistent manipulation, lying and heartless betrayal, the story of Samson and Delilah takes some beating. Samson loves a woman who continually sets out to undermine and control him. His simple, blind love is magnificently expressed in St Saens' opera *Samson and Delilah*—its poignancy moves me to tears.

In time, Delilah brings Samson down. She cuts his hair, which destroys his great strength, then abandons him to the Philistines. They blind and imprison him. End of everything? No, for the Bible whispers at this point, 'But the hair on his head *began to grow again...*' (Judges 16:22). God has ordained that Samson's strength lies in his long hair. No matter what Delilah has done to him, God is already helping Samson, giving him back his strength.

The Bible is realistic about life. It never says that bad relationships won't hurt you. Samson went through a period of misery. You may, too, but God has not forsaken you. He is giving you your strength back, day by day.

God answered Samson's last prayer and the Philistines were indeed put to shame.

Pray with the psalmist: 'You are forgiving and good, O Lord, abounding in love to all who call to you... In the day of my trouble I will call to you... grant your strength to your servant... Give me a sign of your goodness, that my enemies may see it and be put to shame...' (Psalm 86:5–17).

AC

Gifts from God

Don't you see that children are God's best gift?… Like a warrior's fistful of arrows… how blessed are you parents, with your quivers full of children!

A baby really is a totally new beginning and the Bible thinks they are wonderful. Children in the Old Testament are seen as the true riches of a family, unlike material wealth. As for grandchildren, you can't receive a greater blessing than '… may you live to see your children's children' (Psalm 128:6) and Proverbs declares that your 'Children's children are a crown…' (17:6).

However, children are never just accessories, the sole property of the parents who conceive them. Abraham and Sarah knew this of Isaac and Abraham was willing to give his son up when tested. Barren Hannah fasted and prayed for Samuel and then dedicated him back to God when he was born. Children ultimately belong to God.

Nevertheless, parents have major responsibilities towards their children. Babies are adorable and innocent, but the Bible is realistic: no child is born naturally 'good'. 'Folly is bound up in the heart of a child…' (Proverbs 22:15), so no wonder '… a child left to itself disgraces his mother' (Proverbs 29:15). Therefore, our job is to 'Train a child in the way he should go…' (Proverbs 22:6). Parents must also protect their children, never harm them: '… you sacrifice your children in the ravines…' thunders the prophet Isaiah, warning of God's stern judgement (57:5).

What about women who yearn for children and have none? The Lord has compassion on them. He wants to settle '… the barren woman in her home as a happy mother of children' (Psalm 113:9). Whatever this means for individuals, the prophet Isaiah urges, 'Sing, O barren woman, you who never bore a child; burst into song… you who were never in labour; because more are the children of the desolate woman than of her who has a husband…' (54:1). Perhaps the Lord intends that some childless women pour out their mother-love on the many children in desperate need of it.

Ask God to show you if there is a child who could benefit from your love.

AC

How to achieve a new you

Having believed, you were marked in him with a seal, the promised Holy Spirit, who is a deposit guaranteeing our inheritance.

Of course, the biggest new beginning is to be spiritually reborn. Paul declares '... if anyone is in Christ, he is a *new creation*; the old has gone, *the new has come*!' (2 Corinthians 5:17). This new beginning starts when we turn to God, who is actively seeking us in the first place (Philippians 2:12–13) through the Holy Spirit (1 Corinthians 12:3). When we turn to Jesus, he responds by giving us his Spirit, then we are reborn (John 3:6). Rebirth, though, is just the beginning. We have new hope in this life; our inheritance is for eternity (1 Peter 1:3–4).

Have you ever noticed that conversions, like human births, happen in different ways? The New Testament describes four main types, some violent and dramatic (Acts 9:5ff, 10:44ff, 15:7ff, 16:29ff) and some quiet and unspectacular (Acts 8:30ff, 16:14–15).

1. *Sudden crisis conversion:* Think of Saul of Tarsus striding down the Damascus road (Acts 9). Suddenly, he meets Christ. WHAM! Paul's worldview is turned upside down. BOOM! He picks himself up and immediately sets off in a new direction.
2. *Crisis conversion at the end of a process:* Read the story in Acts 8, when Philip leads the already seeking Ethiopian eunuch into eager commitment and baptism.
3. *Series of crises (fits and starts)*: Peter lurched into the kingdom of God. He was bounding along ahead of the other disciples with great affirmations of faith, only to fall flat with his extravagant denials on the night of crucifixion. Yet God, in his mercy, said Peter was a rock and he became the focal point of the early Church.
4. *A gradual process:* The apostle John seems to have had no crises in coming to Jesus. He responded to him from the first and his love and faith in Jesus grew deeper as time went on.

Consider which type of conversion best sums up your experience and thank God for the new life he has given you.

AC

Grow your new beginning

Like newborn babies, crave pure spiritual milk, so that by it you may grow up.

The thing about a new beginning is that you have to build on it—you know the phrase 'use it or lose it'. So, how do you nurture your faith?

First, keep in daily touch with your heavenly Father. Set aside time to pray: 'Do not be anxious about anything, but in everything, by prayer and petition, with thanksgiving, present your requests to God. And the peace of God, which transcends all understanding, will guard your hearts…' (Philippians 4:6–7).

Second, give God a chance to talk back to you. Read the Bible daily, for 'All Scripture is God-breathed…' (2 Timothy 3:16). Take time to think about what you read. Make an effort to grow in your knowledge of God.

Third, be aware that the Holy Spirit is now within you: 'You… are controlled not by the sinful nature but by the Spirit, if the Spirit of God lives in you', declares Paul (Romans 8:9). So, 'Since we live by the Spirit, let us keep in step with the Spirit' (Galatians 5:26). No one can hide their true nature for long, so let the Holy Spirit begin to work in your life, developing your new nature: '… love, joy, peace, patience, kindness, goodness, faithfulness, gentleness and self-control' (Galatians 5:22).

Go to church regularly: 'Let us not give up meeting together… but let us encourage one another…' (Hebrews 10:25). Paul adds, 'Make every effort to keep the unity of the Spirit through the bond of peace…' (Ephesians 4:3).

Witness to your faith: 'Always be prepared to give an answer to everyone who asks you to give the reason for the hope that you have. But do this with gentleness…' (1 Peter 3:15).

Finally, be aware of the spiritual forces aligned against you: 'Be self-controlled and alert. Your enemy the devil prowls around… looking for someone to devour. Resist him, standing firm in the faith…' (1 Peter 5:8–9).

Ask God to highlight anything that might hinder your spiritual growth.

AC

Nine eleven

Where, O death, is your victory? Where, O death, is your sting?

September 11th—the third anniversary of the fall of the Twin Towers in New York; a suitable day for thinking of death and irreplaceable loss.

Surely the toughest of all the new beginnings we might experience is picking up our lives after bereavement. It is unspeakably hard. The death of a loved one leaves such a gaping hole in your life—your own personal Ground Zero, where everything ends.

This new beginning must be made in the valley of the shadow of death and you must make it alone, leaving behind the person you loved. Platitudes are hollow and grating at times like this, but the Bible passages below may speak to your heartache:

'For I am convinced that neither death nor life, neither angels nor demons… nor… anything else in all creation, will be able to separate us from the love of God that is in Christ Jesus our Lord' (Romans 8:37–39).

'If only for this life we have hope in Christ, we are to be pitied more than all men. But… as in Adam all die, so in Christ all will be made alive… The last enemy to be destroyed is death' (1 Corinthians 15:19–26).

'For the perishable must clothe itself with the imperishable, and the mortal with immortality… "Death has been swallowed up in victory"' (1 Corinthians 15:53–54).

'I am the resurrection and the life. He who believes in me will live, even though he dies…' (John 11:25).

Finally, the only way to conclude this series on new beginnings: 'Then I saw a new heaven and a new earth… God… will wipe every tear from their eyes. There will be no more death or mourning or crying or pain, for the old order of things has passed away… He who was seated on the throne said, "I am making *everything new!*"' (Revelation 21:1, 3–5).

Pray with the psalmist: 'The Lord is my shepherd, I shall not be in want… Even though I walk through the valley of the shadow of death, I will fear no evil, for you are with me…' (Psalm 23).

AC

The sacrificing Saviour

He left Judea and departed again to Galilee.
He had to pass through Samaria.

Making a new beginning is never easy because, at some point, the new beginning is well and truly accomplished and we must live with the consequences of the choice we have made. Many who insist adamantly that Jesus was, is and always will be their friend have, sadly, not faced the implications that he must also be accepted as Master and Lord of our lives. Here in John's Gospel is a practical demonstration of the implications of the Lordship of Christ.

Jesus appears to be avoiding the unwanted attentions of the Pharisees. Call it a tactical withdrawal if you will, but I reckon that to infiltrate the alien territory of Samaria deeply, a place where a Jew would definitely be out of his element both culturally and in terms of religious beliefs, was no easy option for anyone. His heavenly Father must have sent him there. He was set on a course to encounter a woman who, without doubt, was in serious need of help. Now is that not a vital characteristic of one worthy of being called Master? He has to be someone who is willing to go anywhere, do anything, sacrifice all, for the sake of those whose lives depend on knowing him. If I am to acknowledge someone as Lord, he has to be proven trustworthy. Jesus has more than proved his worthiness, showing qualities far beyond the capabilities of any mere human being. Christ not only passes through Samaria for his followers but also through the torture of death on a cross and hell itself to carry the pain for us and save our souls.

You once called him friend. You need not fear to accept him as Master and Lord.

Lord, I call you this name so casually sometimes, but I want it to mean exactly that in all its totality. Please teach me to trust your Lordship of my life completely. Bonded to your will, encompassed by your love, engaged in your service, may I discover the freedom that only comes from obedience to you.

HMcD

First contact

There came a woman of Samaria to draw water. Jesus said to her, 'Give me a drink.'

Those who know me know that I am an avid sci-fi enthusiast. My heart beats faster every time the Starship Enterprise prepares to encounter a new life-form. That moment of first contact is the most exciting. Will the creature be friendly or hostile, monstrous or harmless? Will the crew know what to do or will they blow it with crass insensitivity or ignorance of the unknown?

Jesus knew exactly how to approach this alien creature from another country, another culture, tradition and religion, this 'alien' of a different gender. He makes first contact on terms that are familiar to the woman, asking for some water. She feels secure when communication is at this level. A woman at a well in first-century Palestine would have been accustomed to a man expecting her to serve him in this way without any accompanying sinister implications. Jesus, knowing that her need is greater than his, still took time to put her at her ease at their initial meeting.

Nevertheless, for a Jew to even speak to a Samaritan, and a woman at that, filled the lady with amazement (v. 9). She can relax now—he wants her to draw water for him, she knows she is not being solicited. Considering this woman's past, it is a kind and necessary precaution Christ took to begin to fulfil her needs.

See how we can trust him with Lordship! This loving understanding of what we need, and 'where we are at' characterizes all the encounters that Jesus has in the Gospels.

Dear Jesus, thank you for your gentle touch within the relationship of servant/Lord. The world may bully, yet here you are, the Master of the universe, putting yourself in my shoes. Thanks for experiencing the world, the cross, my life. Thank you for approaching me to heal and not hurt further. Teach me to be sensitive to others, learning by your example how to approach with love.

HMcD

Authentic Lordship

'If you knew the gift of God, and who it is that is saying to you, "Give me a drink", you would have asked him, and he would have given you living water.'

Jesus offers to meet the young woman's greatest need—to quench her spiritual thirst—but he makes it very clear that, before such a gift is realized in her life, she must recognize and acknowledge his true nature. What we need comes within our grasp when we acknowledge him as the Christ, the Messiah, the one and only divine Son of the living God who became human for us.

Often we must expel our false Christs and our false conception of God before we can fully trust and believe in Jesus as Lord. Is God a Santa Claus to you? Do your prayers chiefly consist of a shopping list? Is God a tyrant to be feared, born of the wagging finger of our parents who perhaps used him to threaten us with punishment? Perhaps he has become something of the pet dog in our home—the likable, cuddly friend whom we can keep on a lead and take for a walk when we need his company and affection.

Christ refuses to be moulded to fit any of the above shapes. Jesus is co-creator of the universe (John 1:1–4), judge of all the earth (2 Timothy 4:1). He is a king (Hebrews 1:8–9) above all human majesty. It is only by his love and grace that we can have a close relationship with him, despite our failings.

Jesus once asked his disciples, 'But who do you say that I am?' (Luke 9:18–20). Peter got the answer correct (v. 20). I wonder, have we?

Abba, Father, thank you for sending your Son. Forgive us when we try to mould divinity into our own image. Lord, I know you are not a tame God, but, please, draw really close. I do not want to keep you at a distance. Please forgive my mistakes, my sin and my stupidity when I forget who it is I'm talking to.

HMcD

Lord—the author of my being

'Are you greater than our father Jacob who gave us the well, and drank from it himself, and his sons, and his cattle?'

If ever a question revealed a person's priorities and mindset, this one does. The woman bases her security, value system and confidence on her culture/tradition. Her concept of what is right and proper has been gained from past learning—'our father Jacob, and his sons and his cattle'. We in Northern Ireland know more than most the age-old cry, 'We've always done it this way!' She could have echoed, with us, this most dangerous slogan.

Jesus, however, is trying to do a new thing in her life. To accept him as Master and Lord, we have to be prepared for change, letting go of previous areas of security and confidence, putting culture, tradition and possibly our most cherished roots in second place to the call of Christ, admitting that we do not know it all, nor can we succeed by means of our own strength alone. He does not remove anything in order to deprive, but to enrich. We gain much more than we fear of losing when we trust Christ as Lord, but we must be prepared to let go.

To what are we still clinging, imagining that it is our anchor and rock of security when it is really a millstone around our necks, pulling us down and preventing us from rising with Christ? This woman has a great deal of 'baggage' to offload if she is to discover the joy of the Lord. Is she be able to leave it all behind? Are we?

Dear God, forgive me when I allow any thing, person or plan to take first place in my life. Let nothing come before you, my Lord and Master, even when I must relinquish something I consider to be precious. As Lord of my life, may every day reveal to me a new facet of your priceless worth. Rewrite my history, Lord—only then shall I have a history worth living.

HMcD

Lord—the provider

'Sir, give me this water, that I may not thirst, nor come here to draw.'

Oh boy, she still hasn't got it, has she? The Son of the living God is standing there in front of her, offering the most precious gift in the universe and she is trying to save herself the daily physical trek to the well. However, you've got to have a certain amount of sympathy with this woman. From the passage, we know that she has had a life of emotional trauma and is obviously heart-sore from it all. How can we blame her for wanting to grab a chance to reduce the routine grind of water carrying? How often we, too, settle for less—an immediate short-term fix rather than eternal blessings.

Her appetite is still focused on herself, her thirst, her effort, her future responsibilities to bring home the water. Has she lifted her eyes from the mundane bucket to look properly into the face of Jesus yet? How many water carriers trek daily to wells that neither refresh nor satisfy? The Lordship of Christ promises to alter our course, reshuffle our priorities and revitalize our purpose. It brings us hope of true satisfaction.

Jesus, having gradually, with patience, nurtured the conversation with the woman, is now about to put his finger on the crux of the matter for her. Will she be strong enough to face it and find him without embarrassment or fear? Will she know the degree of her thirst? Do we? The Lordship of Christ means that he has to set the terms and conditions of the agreement, not us.

Dear Lord, your provision never falls short of my extensive needs. Thank you. Help me to bring each need to you without fear. Help me to identify real needs without greed. Help me to enjoy your provision without lapsing into ingratitude. May each day that passes mature my palate to desire spiritual satisfaction, rather than merely having my material needs met. Thanks, Lord, for knowing the full extent of my needs in every respect.

HMcD

Lord—who cleanses

'Go, call your husband, and come here.'

Once more, how tenderly the Lord broaches the awkward subject of her sin. There is no instant and brutal sledgehammer of condemnation, no name calling. Instead, he gives the woman an opportunity to voluntarily reveal her situation. She answers truthfully, 'I have no husband' (v. 17). 'You are right... for you have had five husbands, and he whom you now have is not your husband...' (vv. 17–18). Jesus even congratulates her on her honesty.

My belief that this interchange is spoken in a spirit of compassion and not one of loud accusation is bolstered by her next comment: 'Sir, I perceive that you are a prophet' (v. 19). Had Jesus wagged the finger of scorn she would surely have run, insulted. Instead she stays to hear more, and already a bridge has been forged between them.

The Lord is not sparing the knife that will cut the cancer of sin from her soul, yet she wants to know more. Nevertheless, she attempts to hide behind their theological and cultural differences (v. 20). Perhaps it was her way of changing the subject or maybe she raises this important issue between Samaritans and Jews to push him to the furthermost point of his indulgence. Most Jews would have been distracted into an explosion of defensiveness regarding their traditional position. Red herrings are Satan's most versatile weapons and he continues today to use them to tempt many into avoiding the central claims of the Lordship of Christ, both outside the Church and, sadly, within it. Maybe she wants to learn more, but without the embarrassment of further probing into her personal situation.

However, the Lordship of Christ is not merely theological—it is about a relationship between himself and us; it is intensely personal. Jesus supersedes both traditional stances in one fell swoop by highlighting the central issue of worship, which is not where, but whom she should worship (v. 24).

Father, forgive my distractions and all avoidance tactics. Keep my eyes focused on the right priorities; I want to see Jesus.

HMcD

Lord Messiah

Jesus said to her, 'I who speak to you am he.'

The woman has faith that the Messiah is coming (v. 25) and expresses her staunch belief that he will reveal all things. No need to tread on tiptoe now, Lord, we urge. Jesus then makes one of the most unequivocal statements of his true nature in the Gospels: 'I who speak to you am he.'

Isn't it interesting that at this point in the chapter, on what modern films might designate a cliffhanger, John breaks away from the narrative to tell us that the disciples suddenly arrive back from the shops (v. 27)? It must have had a significant impact on those disciples to return to Jesus with the food he had sent them to buy (v. 8), only to find him breaking not one but several taboos. He was talking to a Samaritan—a woman at that—what a shock! A clever little trick of Satan's is to attempt to distract someone right on the point of their making a commitment to Christ and here the woman is distracted by the reaction of the returning disciples.

The devil is wily indeed. First he tried theological arguments, then he attempted a diversion of disdain towards the woman, with the chance of throwing her temporarily back into the feelings of shame and guilt that Jesus was intent on healing. Does he try the same tactics with us? The woman abandoned her water jar (v. 28). She must have run in joy to the city for she says, 'Come, see a man who told me all that I ever did. Can this be Christ?' (v. 29). We are told that 'Many Samaritans from that city believed in him because of the woman's testimony' (vv. 39–42).

Meanwhile, back at the well, the disciples were left to face their prejudice, intolerance and religious arrogance—their shock being the very reason the story managed to find its way into the Gospel narrative. A cautionary tale indeed for us all.

Lord, Messiah, to have it recorded that many believed because of my testimony would be the greatest joy of all. I pray it will be so.

HMcD

Hosea the prophet

When the Lord began to speak through Hosea...

Hosea is a wonderful book, rich in meaning and powerful images. I admit that it is not an easy read. Much of the original text is hard to understand, partly because it is written in a dialect of the north—Hosea was a northerner, part of the northern kingdom. Much of the meaning of the text is hidden, couched in poetry and symbolism, but don't let that put you off—the treasure in God's word is often hidden.

Jesus spoke in parables so that those who thought they knew it all could not, and would not, understand. Many turn their back on Christianity today because they don't understand its wonderful message of grace, freedom and forgiveness. Anything that is worth having is worth making an effort for.

Hosea really is a wonderful book with a truly remarkable message—the Lord of all, the God of justice and holiness, may have every reason to be angry with us, but he loves us with a love that breaks his heart; a love that pours out grace and mercy; a love that will not let us go.

The first three chapters of Hosea tell the story of Hosea's marriage to an unfaithful wife, Gomer. Chapters 4—14 contain prophesies that echo the theme of Israel's unfaithfulness and God's reaction to it.

I have learnt much as I have studied the book of Hosea in preparation for writing these notes. Come with me on a journey to learn more about our God, who is both just and loving. We will also hear from Hosea himself as we study his book. Do read the full Bible verses suggested to make the most of these notes.

Is there anything you think God might ask you to do that you shy away from because it seems difficult? Pray that you will have the courage to tackle any task that lies ahead of you.

Lord, thank you for your love that is unfailing, unconditional and undeserved. Help me to live each day with increasing awareness of your love.

KP

Hosea who?

The word of the Lord that came to Hosea son of Beeri during the reigns of Uzziah, Jotham, Ahaz and Hezekiah, kings of Judah, and during the reign of Jeroboam son of Joash king of Israel.

Who was Hosea? The fact is, we know very little about him. The first verse does not give much of a clue. The kings mentioned tell us that he lived around 760BC. He overlaps with Isaiah, Micah (both prophets of the southern kingdom), and the events of 2 Kings and 2 Chronicles. His time of prophecy spans the reign of Jeroboam II and the turbulent years after his death.

Why are four Judean kings named, but only one king of Israel? This is because Hosea is a prophet of the northern kingdom, of Israel, not Judah in the south.

Maybe I am asking the wrong questions. Maybe Hosea wasn't interested in historical details or telling us much about himself. The book starts with the words 'The word of the Lord...' and that is what it is all about!

Who will still remember us in 100 years' time? In 200 years? Who will still read what I have written in ten years, even one year? This is a sobering thought, but not a negative one. What we do is fleeting, but it doesn't mean that we don't count. Think of those who are famous and will be remembered in 100 years' time. Are they any more important than you and I?

God's economy is different. We are here on earth because he wants us to be and because he wants to use us. Our impact on this world is linked to our obedience to him. It doesn't matter whether we are a 'somebody' in the world's eyes or no one knows our name. We are a somebody in God's eyes. He knows our name and what impact he has on others through us. It doesn't matter that we don't know much about Hosea. We can learn more about God through Hosea and that's what matters.

Read Isaiah 62:1–3 to find out how God sees you.

KP

Unfaithfulness

'Go, take to yourself an adulterous wife and children of unfaithfulness, because the land is guilty of the vilest adultery in departing from the Lord.' So he married Gomer.

A spirit of prostitution leads them astray; they are unfaithful to their God.

Israel has turned away from the one true God and allowed its own religion to be watered down by accepting Canaanite gods and the fertility cult prevalent in that society. The God of Israel and Baal are treated almost in the same way. As the religion of Canaan involves shrine prostitutes, Israel is engaged in both literal and spiritual unfaithfulness.

We can imagine Hosea saying, 'I have to marry Gomer because the Lord told me so, and I cannot be disobedient, but it's more than that. I love Gomer. I know she is a wonderful woman—beautiful, kind, loving. I see her go off with other men… I long for her to leave her life of unfaithfulness, to turn back to me. She thinks she is pursuing happiness but she will never find true joy, running from one pleasure to the next, never content. Can't she see what she is doing to me? Doesn't she care? Lord, why do I have to go through this? Will Israel learn from this example? Will Gomer ever learn? Gomer, come back!'

Hosea's marriage to Gomer is a parable acted out, showing how Israel has treated God. God longs for his people to return to him at least as much as Hosea longs for Gomer to come back.

We are not unfaithful, of course. We don't turn to other gods—television, status, money, good jobs or even the more subtle ones of a prominent role in church or doing lots of good works. The change from worshipping God to worshipping something that is *of* God is subtle. I'm not advocating that we should become paranoid about our motives for the good works we do. It might just be good to ask ourselves occasionally what, or who, is most important to us.

What does God feel when he looks at us, our family, our nation?

KP

A God of justice and mercy

'Call him Jezreel, because I will soon punish the house of Jehu for the massacre at Jezreel, and I will put an end to the kingdom of Israel.'

I will tear them to pieces and go away.

Gomer has had a baby boy and God has told Hosea to call the child Jezreel, referring to the massacre mentioned in 2 Kings 9.

What might Hosea say? 'God has given us a beautiful baby boy and we have had to call him Jezreel. Anyone who meets the boy will always be reminded of the massacre. My poor boy, he will be a reminder to his people of these terrible events, this dreadful sin. Israel thought God had forgotten, but God does not forget. God knows what is in the heart of his people. We are all doomed.'

These verses make for uncomfortable reading. God threatens to punish his people, to tear them to pieces even. What do we make of so much violence?

I like to think of God as my loving Father. In fact, I know he is loving for he has shown himself to be so many times. Yet, I am a sinner as well; we all are. God is a holy God and he cannot tolerate unholiness. He is a just God. He has every reason to be angry and to want to punish Israel. He has every reason to punish us.

That is not the whole story. Hosea's acted parable is not finished yet. Israel's story is not finished either. The Lord is a God of justice—and of mercy. God loves Israel so much that he cannot leave his people to live a life of sinfulness. He threatens not in order to punish, but to shake them into action. All Israel needs to do is repent. All we need do is repent. God awaits us with outstretched arms, as Hosea 6:1 affirms.

Lord, forgive us our sins, as we forgive those who sin against us.

KP

Taken for granted

'Call her Lo-Ruhamah, for I will no longer show love to the house of Israel, that I should at all forgive them.'

Israel has forgotten his Maker and built palaces; Judah has fortified many towns.

'God has given us a baby daughter and we have had to call her Lo-Ruhamah, which means "not loved", but I love my little daughter—how can I call her "not loved"? I can see what the Lord is saying. We have tried his patience and it has run out. We have taken him for granted. Israel thought God would always be on their side, that he would always keep his side of the covenant, even if his people did not keep theirs. Israel has relied on palaces and fortresses. We are no longer loved by God!' Hosea is desperate. The Lord is angry. Can God's love ever run out?

I recently met a fairly new Christian. It was less than a year since she had found God, in a rather dramatic fashion, during her brother's baptism service. She had only gone to please him. She almost didn't make it as she had been abroad until the day before and her flight back was delayed due to fog. Eleven months on, she was planning to celebrate the anniversary of her new life in Christ. She was full of enthusiasm and the fire of her love for God was very evident.

It made me think. I have been a Christian for most of my life. My journey to knowledge of the living God has been a gradual one that took all my childhood and teenage years—a journey of increasing understanding with increasing age. I don't have the same fire as this new Christian. Am I taking God for granted? Am I in danger of putting my security elsewhere, building fortresses that might not be made of stone but of job security and pension plans?

Lord, you are amazing! Thank you for the miracle of your loving us enough to die for us.

KP

Choices

Then the Lord said, 'Call him Lo-Ammi, for you are not my people, and I am not your God.'

'An eagle is over the house of the Lord because the people have broken my covenant and rebelled against my law.'

'She made me do it', cried Joe. 'He started it!' exclaimed Sarah. 'I can't help it! It's my upbringing/circumstances/surroundings.' 'Everybody does it.' 'You have to be cruel to be kind.' 'It's not my fault.'

It's easy, isn't it? If in doubt, blame someone else or, even better, something else that can't answer back. We've all done it and not only as children… I certainly have.

Gomer has had another child—a son—and God has told Hosea to name his new baby Lo-Ammi, meaning 'not my people', for God is no longer their God. In fact, he says 'I am no longer your I AM', echoing the language used in Exodus when the covenant between God and his people started. The covenant is broken, the married couple (God and Israel) are divorced. Is it God's fault?

God loves Israel with a love that is fiercer than any love they can imagine. In the same way, he loves us with a love beyond our wildest dreams. He loves us so much that he has given us a precious gift—freedom. The Israelites had freedom of choice and chose to break the covenant. Later, they thought better of it, as we shall see. We, too, have a choice. Life can be wonderful; life can be tough. We can choose to respond to whatever life throws at us. God does not force us to go down the right path—he allows us to make our own choices, even if he knows that we will hurt others and ourselves. He does not force us to love him either. He is waiting for us with outstretched arms. We have a choice to make.

Read Luke 15:11–24 for an example of the consequence of love and freedom. Respond to God with a heart of love and trust him to lead you.

KP

Different kinds of riches

She said, 'I will go after my lovers who give me my food and my water, my wool and my linen, my oil and my drink.'

Ephraim boasts, 'I am very rich; I have become wealthy. With all my wealth they will not find in me any iniquity or sin.'

Sue lives in a large house in a beautiful village close to Oxford. She drives a sports car. She has a good job. She spent last Easter at a health farm with a few friends, being pampered. She has meals out, goes to parties, enjoys herself. She comes across as confident, exuberant, someone who enjoys life. She has everything she ever aimed for.

Sue is not enjoying her job, but dare not give it up as she has a large mortgage. The sports car looks great but is not very comfortable to drive. Her social life leaves her empty. She wonders about giving it all up, changing jobs, moving to a smaller house, getting a more practical car... She wonders whether or not her high-flying friends will still accept her without the house and the car and the salary. She has everything she ever aimed for, but wonders, 'Is that really what I've always wanted?'

Gomer goes after her lovers because they promise her what she needs or thinks she needs. Ephraim (a word for the north of Israel) equals wealth with righteousness.

To be perfectly honest, I quite envy Sue sometimes. Sometimes I think I wouldn't mind her house (I live as a lodger and my bedroom window overlooks a council estate) or her car (I have a bike!) or a weekend being pampered. I wouldn't mind her confidence. Sue seemingly has everything and appears happy but is aching inside. She does not know Jesus. Maybe I don't envy her after all. I have everything I really need and I have the greatest treasure of all—Jesus.

Thank you, Father, that your promises are true: '... I have come that they may have life, and have it to the full' (John 10:10).

KP

God as an insurance policy?

Then she will say, 'I will go back to my husband as at first, for then I was better off than now.' She has not acknowledged that I was the one who gave her the grain, the new wine and oil, who lavished on her the silver and gold—which they used for Baal.

'Come, let us return to the Lord. He has torn us to pieces but he will heal us.'

'Become a Christian and your life will instantly be better! Happiness, financial security, health, good social life, no more worries. Walk in God's ways and all your problems will disappear. Join this church and we will show you how.' Really?

Being a Christian is great. It certainly improves your social life. If you join a good church (like mine!), you gain a great support network. What about those uncomfortable verses on suffering, though?

Jesus did not say: 'I have come that they may have a comfortable life, free from pain and suffering, with continuous happiness and prosperity.' Jesus promised us life in all its fullness and I believe that means life with all its joy and pain. Pain and suffering are part of life. Life is more than merely existing. If we are truly alive, we will have the capacity to feel joy but also to feel pain.

Whenever I am in danger of envying people like Sue (see yesterday's reading) I think back to my trip to Tanzania in 2002 and remember the joyfulness of the Christians I met there—Christians who live in mud huts and have to fetch water from the river. Their life is hard, without much hope of improvement. They have nothing in material terms, yet radiate the joy of knowing Jesus; the joy of being alive. They know that every good thing in their life comes from God.

Think about all the good things that God has given to you and, as you go about doing today's tasks, spend time thanking him for them.

KP

The desert

'Therefore I am now going to allure her; I will lead her into the desert and speak tenderly to her.'

'Ephraim is like a dove, easily deceived and senseless, now calling to Egypt, now turning to Assyria.'

Excuse me? You want to lead me into the desert? Into a hot and barren place, where there is no water, food, shade, comfort, and you expect me to follow you? You can keep your tender words for a nicer place!

If Gomer (or Israel for that matter) had known about God's plan for desert walking, she would have been forgiven for thinking she didn't want to go. The desert can be beautiful for a short while, provided you carry adequate equipment but, generally speaking, the desert is not a place where anyone would choose to stay for any length of time. This was certainly the case for the Israelites—their ancestors had already spent 40 years in the desert, after all.

The verses from Hosea 7 talk about Israel's foolish foreign policy. Ephraim (Israel) tries to get in with its larger, stronger neighbours, aligning themselves first with Assyria, then with Egypt. Both are countries that pose a threat to Israel. God uses this threat and the difficulties that arise with it to shake Israel into action. Gomer is led into the desert, stripped of all other distractions and possessions, so that she will come to her senses.

The desert is not a nice place. We will all have our personal desert experiences at some time or other in life. Sometimes, God can use desert times to remove all our imagined security and draw us closer to him. A friend once wrote a note to me after we had both gone through a difficult time: 'This is the place where God refines us, painful though it may be.'

Pray for anyone you know who is going through a difficult time. Pray for yourself if that's you. You may like to read Psalm 23, slowly, drinking in the familiar words that assure us of God's care.

KP

It breaks my heart!

'Love her [your wife] as the Lord loves the Israelites, though they turn to other gods and love the sacred raisin cakes.'

When Israel was a child, I loved him, and out of Egypt I called my son. But the more I called Israel, the further they went from me.

Imagine Hosea speaking: 'It breaks my heart! God has told me to take Gomer back, even though he knows and I know that she is going after other men. I have bought her back and told her to leave the others. It pains me to think of what she has done; how she has turned away from me, thinking she could buy happiness, thinking that others were giving her what she wants, but it was me who looked after her all the time. How could she be so blind? I love her so much that I will take her back, despite everything. I just hope that she she will really turn back to me. Oh Gomer!'

Have you ever loved someone so much that this love has made your heart ache? Have you ever seen a loved one turn away from all that is good and go down their own destructive path, leaving you to watch helplessly, praying for them to turn around? The sacred raisin cakes referred to here were used in Baal fertility rites. Loving them meant Israel had turned away from God.

Liz and Ben had been engaged for a while. They were both Christians, happy to be together, happy to know God. Then Ben turned away. He wasn't sure he wanted to marry Liz after all. He wasn't sure he believed in God any more. He found another woman, not a Christian, and went off with her. Liz waited and prayed. Then, the miracle happened—the prodigal came to his senses. Ben returned to Liz and, most importantly, to God. It is never too late to turn around.

This is how God feels whenever any of his children reject him. Pray for any known to you who have turned away from God.

KP

Old habits die hard

The Israelites are stubborn, like a stubborn heifer. How then can the Lord pasture them like lambs in a meadow? Ephraim is joined to idols; leave him alone!

Martin and Liz have just moved back to the UK after four years in South America. They are finding their feet again in their home country, but it has lost its familiarity after the four years they spent abroad: 'We feel startled to find people speaking English in the street. We expect them to speak Spanish. We expect to have difficulties communicating.'

They have moved into a lovely new house, but everything is unfamiliar. 'Where is the washing-up liquid? How do I work this cooker? Where are those plates? Oh no, they are in the container that is still on its way back to the UK!'

Moving house—and even more so when moving country—makes you realize how you take familiar things for granted. Habits form quickly. You expect things to be a certain way. This is normal and even healthy, up to a point, but the Israelites had got into some very unhealthy habits. They had taken on the religion and customs of the Canaanites and these had become so familiar to them that they seemed normal. Israel could not break the habit. Maybe they didn't even want to!

The more frequently and more intensively we do something, the more it becomes a habit and the harder it is to change our ways. This is true for negative things—overeating, overworking, overspending, watching mindless TV programmes, even having a negative attitude. The good news is that this is also true for positive things—healthy eating, making time for the children, praying, using Bible-reading notes, having a positive attitude.

The Israelites had got into some very bad habits but, with God, there is always hope; always a chance for change.

Are there any habits that you want to change? Are there any habits you want to strengthen? Share your needs with a friend, pray for each other and keep each other accountable as you develop new habits.

KP

To know God

I know all about Ephraim; Israel is not hidden from me…
A spirit of prostitution is their heart;
they do not acknowledge the Lord.

I will betroth you in faithfulness,
and you will acknowledge the Lord.

What a contrast between these two verses! Hosea 5:4 talks about the Israelites not acknowledging God. Hosea 2:20 shows a husband talking tenderly to his beloved, like Hosea would to Gomer or God to the Israelites.

To know and to be known; to be acknowledged, are basic desires for every human being. A newborn baby forms its identity in relation to its mother or the person who looks after it most of the time. After a few months, the baby discovers that it is separate, a person in its own right. As the child grows older, it becomes more and more independent, yet it needs the security of contact with its parent or carer. The child needs to know and to be known to form its own identity. In fact, I shouldn't refer to the child as 'it' but as 'she' or 'he' for, of course, the child is a person, known and acknowledged by God, even before he or she is aware of it.

The Israelites had lost this knowledge. God knew them all right, but Israel did not know, or want to know, God. The Israelites were looking for their identity elsewhere, among other gods.

Where are we getting our identity from? Society tells us that we are what we do and what we have. 'What do you do? What car do you drive? Where do you live? Are you married? Single? Divorced? Do you have children? Well, then I can tell you who you are.' Actually, forget the job and the car. Even the children can't give us an identity. Only God can. He knows us. We know him. Who are you? A daughter of the King.

Lord, thank you that you know me and accept me as I am. Thank you for the privilege of knowing you. Give me the courage to acknowledge you at all times.

KP

True worship

For I desire mercy, not sacrifice, and acknowledgement of God rather than burnt offerings.

Jesus said, 'It is not the healthy who need a doctor, but the sick. But go and learn what this means: "I desire mercy, not sacrifice." For I have not come to call the righteous, but sinners.'

Jesus says these words after the Pharisees have asked his disciples why their master had dinner with tax collectors and sinners. The Pharisees think that they have sussed it all out: there are good people and bad people. They are the good people and the tax collectors the bad ones. There can be no doubt about which is which. Then Jesus comes along and actually seeks the company of sinners. How could he?!

The problem is obviously not new. Some 800 years before this incident, God has something to say to the Israelites. They turn to him when it suits them and bring a few burnt offerings, thinking this will please the Lord, but their 'love is like the morning mist' (Hosea 6:4) and doesn't last. God is not after a showy outward display of religion. He knows the heart. God desires mercy—*hésed*—a word that can also be translated as covenant faithfulness.

Gone are the days when it was the done thing to go to church. However, even today there are church stalwarts who don't believe in God. Even today there are those who mistake going to church and doing certain things as pleasing to God. Even today, there are churches where they think that they have found the right formula for approaching the Lord of Hosts. It is so easy to mistake forms of worship for true worship. The shift can be subtle, almost unnoticeable.

The good news is that we don't need to be good at anything. It is enough to simply come to God. What he asks is easy, but it may be the hardest thing of all to do: God wants our heart.

Lord, I give you all I am; all I have been and all I long to be.

KP

All shall be well

Bow and sword and battle I will abolish from the land, so that all may lie down in safety.

I will be like dew to Israel; he will blossom like a lily.

'Do you sometimes wonder if there's life on other planets?' asks eight-year-old Michael. In the background, the radio is on with the news: 200 people killed in the latest bomb attack in one country. Renewed fighting in another country. Little girl found dead on wasteland near her home. In response, his sister Laura says, 'I sometimes wonder why there is life on *this* planet.'

A poignant story? This world is far from happy and perfect. We fight, lie, steal, think mainly of ourselves. Christians are no exception. Don't you long for a world where everyone can live in peace?

God loves us passionately. He loves us so much that he has given us freedom—freedom to make our own choices, to make mistakes, mess things up. I am not trying to give an answer to the question 'Why is there suffering and killing in this world?', but I have learnt something from studying the book of Hosea: God loves us more than we can ever imagine. He loves us so much that it breaks his heart. He longs for a response from us. Whether or not we do respond, his love will hold on to us. His is a love that will not let us go.

The Lord of all has reason to be angry, for he is a holy and just God. The Lord who sent his Son to die for us is a God of mercy and grace. He loves us fiercely. A life worth living is a life acknowledging him. Total freedom comes from serving him. One day, God will wipe every tear from our eyes (Revelation 21:4). In the meantime, let us aim to make this world a better place.

Nothing can separate us from the love of God (Romans 8:39). Read the whole of Romans 8:38–39, and thank God that we are secure in his love.

KP

King of the Jews

After Jesus was born in Bethlehem in Judea, during the time of King Herod, Magi from the east came to Jerusalem and asked, 'Where is the one who has been born king of the Jews? We saw his star in the east and have come to worship him.'

King of kings and Lord of lords. All hail King Jesus. He's the King of the jungle... Our hymns and songs are peppered with references to Jesus as king. Our theology, too, proclaims his kingship: we are members of his kingdom. We invite his reign over our lives and pray that his kingdom will come. Jesus equals king.

So what does that mean? Over the next few days, we will take a quick dip into Matthew's Gospel for some clues. What did it mean to Jesus that he was 'born king of the Jews'? What sort of king is he? What is his kingdom like? Also, of course, the million-dollar question, what does Jesus being king mean to each of us?

Over 2000 years ago, a king was what the Jews were hoping for. They were looking for a ruler of their own, as Israel was controlled by Herod the Great, a puppet of the Romans. Under Herod, the Jews were not a happy bunch. Living in occupied territory, they longed for deliverance. They needed a hero to beat the Romans and set them free. They wanted their country back.

How extraordinary that it was star-studying foreigners who knew that a new king had indeed been born. They must have caused chaos in Herod's court. This despot had no compunction in disposing of his nearest and dearest when he felt threatened. How much more a suspected king.

Right from the start, then, Jesus' kingship caused trouble. As we think about this further, let your own reactions draw you closer to the one who really is the King of kings and Lord of lords.

Read Matthew 27:11 and respond. Lord, thank you that you are king. Help me to discover more of what that means for me.

DA

Expecting a king

'The virgin will be with child and will give birth to a son, and they will call him Immanuel'—which means, "God with us"... 'Bethlehem... out of you will come a ruler who will be the shepherd of my people Israel.'

These are familiar words to those of us used to celebrating Christmas as Christians. They may well conjure up candlelight, mince pies and soul-warming music. These words that Matthew was quoting come from Isaiah and Micah. For the Jews of Jesus' time, they must have triggered longing. Surely those Jews scoured their scriptures for promises of deliverance by their God. In such difficult, nation-threatening circumstances, they must have been desperate for reassurance that God would come through for them again. Matthew, writing for his fellow Jews, was at pains to point out to them that, in Jesus, all those prophecies were fulfilled.

Perhaps it is not surprising that the Jews did not instantly recognize Jesus as their king. After all, their most famous king, David, was a brilliant military commander and inspired political ruler. Wasn't that what they needed again? Jesus' ministry attracted increasing crowds and was obviously powerful—many saw miracles when they were around him. However, Jesus would not be drawn into the political agendas of his day. John's Gospel records for us the day that Jesus just disappeared into the mountains when his fellow Jews tried to declare him king (John 6:14–15).

Were some of the Jews disappointed? Jesus consistently refused to be swayed by the expectations of those around him. He stuck to his job description. Do we, too, come to Jesus the King with expectations? Do we fail to see what he is doing in our lives because we are blinded by our own agendas? Are we ever—dare I suggest—disappointed by him? The Jews who turned away from Jesus missed out on the greatest story ever told. How can we be open to who Jesus really is and keep following him?

Read Proverbs 20:28 and thank God for the power of love.

DA

The king's father

Then Jesus came from Galilee to the Jordan to be baptized by John... As soon as Jesus was baptized... heaven was opened, and he saw the Spirit of God descending like a dove and lighting on him. And a voice from heaven said, 'This is my Son, whom I love; with him I am well pleased.'

While the Jews around him struggled to accept who Jesus was, Jesus himself had no such problem. Unlike many of us, he seemed to know who he was, why he was here and what he was here to do. Publicly, it all began here, at Jesus' baptism. He was affirmed and acknowledged by the words from his Father, by the anointing of the Spirit, and his ministry exploded into life from this point. I love the fact that God told him how pleased he was with him before Jesus' public work even began.

So, right from the start, Jesus was not king on his own. Instead, he was in an intimate and secure relationship with God that was based on love and affirmation. His work flowed from this. His very being was about relationship; he had nothing to prove. His father was already king.

The obvious point to make here is that surely this should be a model for us? Isn't the challenge here for us, too, to become so secure in our relationship with our heavenly Father that we can also experience his love and affirmation without us having to do a thing? Instead, we get caught up in trying to prove to God—and ourselves—that we are worth it. We treat life as if it were an examination and forget to live in the grace and freedom God offers. Yet we are children of God, adopted into his family. If so, isn't God pleased with us, too?

I get the impression that God was enjoying Jesus at his baptism. Can we let him enjoy us as well and relax into the affirmation that brings us?

Thank God for the intimacy reflected in Psalm 139.

DA

Kingly temptations

Then Jesus was led by the Spirit into the desert to be tempted by the devil… the devil took him to a very high mountain and showed him all the kingdoms of the world and their splendour. 'All this I will give you,' he said, 'if you will bow down and worship me.' Jesus said to him, 'Away from me, Satan! For it is written: "Worship the Lord your God, and serve him only."'

I have a theory that secretly we think that, because Jesus is God's Son, it is easier for him to resist temptations than it ever is for us. He is God, after all. He is stronger than us. That can't be true, though, or they wouldn't be real temptations. These foodless 40 days in the desert are somehow vital to Jesus' ministry, just as his baptism has been. It is the Spirit who leads him into the desert, just as it is the Spirit who comes to him just before in baptism.

Painful thoughts really. I don't like to think of God allowing people to be tested with temptations. Even Jesus. So why was it necessary? Jesus has just experienced the warmth of his baptismal affirmation from God. Now he is hungry, alone and facing the devil. This final temptation speaks directly to the type of king he is called to be. The devil is offering him the easy way. 'Compromise', says the devil, 'just a bit of worship and I will let you reign over all the kingdoms of the world.'

There's another painful thought: the devil rules over the kingdoms of the world. Something to bear in mind when reading the newspaper. Yet, Jesus knows that God still has the ultimate authority and proves it by throwing Deuteronomy 6:13 at the devil like a punch. The devil retreats. Jesus has won. He faces the devil again throughout his ministry, but his colours are nailed firmly to his Father's mast. He is going God's way to kingship, not anyone else's.

How do you cope with temptation? Take comfort from Hebrews 2:14–18.

DA

The obedient, unexpected king

'Do not think that I have come to abolish the Law or the Prophets; I have not come to abolish them but to fulfil them.'

The aim of the Law and the prophets was to call people into a place of obedience to God's will. This is something Jesus does naturally and decisively. In obedience, Jesus began his ministry. In obedience, he began to preach, teach and heal. Not surprisingly, the crowds begin to gather. They begin asking themselves who he is. If he is not a David-style king, what sort of king is he?

Intriguingly, he is a king who talks about God in a new way. The crowds are enthralled. Jesus claims to know the Father intimately (Matthew 11:27) and only to do what his Father tells him. Later he is obedient even to death.

However, this obedience doesn't make him a yes man. We have already seen him strong in the face of temptation. As he goes about Palestine, he stirs up controversy just by being who he is and refusing to compromise with expectations, pressure to conform or even social niceties. How would you have felt if Jesus had sent your herd of pigs over a cliff to get rid of demons in a man? What if it was your money that scattered over the temple floor as Jesus threw over the tables? Do you really want to hear that it is easier for a camel to get through the eye of a needle than for a rich man to get into the kingdom of God? Why on earth does Jesus cause the fig tree to wither?

This King Jesus may not wield a sword or raise an army, but he is no less powerful. The question for us has to be: do we try to keep Jesus how we want him to be or meet him as he really is?

Bring to God one of the scenes from Jesus' life that you struggle to understand and ask God to show you how he was obedient to the Father in it.

DA

The compassionate king

Jesus went through all the towns and villages, teaching in their synagogues, preaching the good news of the kingdom and healing every disease and sickness. When he saw the crowds, he had compassion on them, because they were harassed and helpless, like sheep without a shepherd.

I don't know about you, but I have plenty of days when I feel harassed and helpless, so this compassionate side of Jesus' kingship is something I relate to and, indeed, covet. Isn't it reassuring that Jesus saw the people in the crowds as they really were? When you are in a crowd, you think it doesn't show that you are feeling like a limp lettuce, but Jesus sees.

We, as his followers, can easily major on one aspect of ministry. Some of us are good at teaching, some at preaching, some at healing in one way or another and so on, but Jesus can do it all. He dealt with people in an authentically holistic way. He challenged their minds, nurtured their souls and healed their bodies. Who wouldn't want a king like that?

There is just one detail: in order to benefit from the compassionate nature of our king, we have to admit to needing his touch. Whether I am having a limp lettuce day or a strong oak tree day, I still have to admit my need. Think of the people Jesus healed—unless they were unable to for some reason, they asked for their healing. There was that poor sick woman who crept up to grab the hem of his robe. There was the blind man who yelled from the side of the road. There was the centurion who asked on behalf of his daughter. They all asked.

What holds us back from asking Jesus for what we need? Foolish pride? Thinking we have to cope on our own? Doubt that he will help us? This is why we need good theology. We need to be convinced of both our own dependency on God and the unfailing compassionate nature of our king. Then we need to experience it.

Go ahead—ask.

DA

The servant king

'Here is my servant whom I have chosen, the one I love, in whom I delight; I will put my Spirit on him, and he will proclaim justice to the nations. He will not quarrel or cry out; no one will hear his voice in the streets. A bruised reed he will not break, and a smouldering wick he will not snuff out, till he leads justice to victory. In his name the nations will put their hope.'

This wonderful passage that Matthew quotes from Isaiah reinforces for us that Jesus did not come to lord it over anybody. Isaiah emphasizes the opposite: Jesus came to serve.

It is an amazing thing that the creator of the world chose to come to serve his creation. I wonder how far we have understood it. Thinking of yesterday's verses and the invitation to come to Jesus and ask for what we need is challenging enough, but when I think of Jesus as a servant, there is something within me that struggles with the concept. Could it be that in our celebrity-dominated age we are happier when those we admire are on a pedestal? Could it be that I want to keep Jesus on one, just slightly out of my reach? Do you remember when Jesus took a bowl of water and towel and insisted on cleaning his disciples' feet at the Last Supper (John 13)? I know I would have protested, just like Peter did. It was a servant's job! How could I receive such a thing from my Lord?

Is it just me or do others also find the thought of Jesus kneeling in front of us in order to serve just a mite tricky? Picture it now. How do you respond to this humble, gentle, tender Jesus? Do you want to resist or can you relax and allow Jesus to minister to you? He was adamant that his disciples needed it. I guess we do, too.

Lord, sometimes I am that bruised reed.
I have dirty feet.
I need you to serve me—but!
It's hard.
Help me receive from you, my kneeling king.

DA

The grateful king

When Jesus came into Peter's house, he saw Peter's mother-in-law lying in bed with a fever. He touched her hand and the fever left her, and she got up and began to wait on him.

Here is Jesus practising what he preaches. As well as expecting us to receive from him, he is also able to receive from others. On this occasion, Peter's mother-in-law made him food, after herself receiving a miraculous healing, but this was far from an isolated incident. Jesus was dependent on others for most of his ministry as he travelled around. He had no home to return to and we know that he was supported financially by others, including many women (Luke 8:3). He was obviously a welcome visitor in Mary and Martha's home and he frequently ate at others' houses. He borrowed a room for the Last Supper. He was a king, but he was happy to receive.

Not many of us are kings, yet we can find it as hard to receive from others around us as we do from Jesus himself. So much of Western culture in particular encourages a go-it-alone, individualistic outlook that discourages us from willingly receiving from others. To live is to cope. Success is to look like a success, no matter how bad you feel underneath. To be human is to have it all together.

Is that really what we were made for? Isolated islands shouting to one another that we are 'Fine, thanks' when really we are wondering how we are going to get through another day? Jesus was the ultimate 'together' person, but he gave and received happily, withdrew when he was tired and slept in a boat while his friends did the rowing. If we are made for relationship rather than isolation, then we need to depend on others, too, just like Jesus did. It was probably one of the things that kept him so together.

Lord, help me to receive from others when I need to. Deal with my insecurities and make me like you. Meditate on Matthew 26:6–13.

DA

The anti-king?

'Blessed are the poor in spirit, for theirs is the kingdom of heaven. Blessed are those who mourn, for they will be comforted. Blessed are the meek, for they will inherit the earth. Blessed are those who hunger and thirst for righteousness, for they will be filled.'

These words are from the beginning of what is known as the Beatitudes, from the Sermon on the Mount. What a strange manifesto for a kingdom! Here is a topsy-turvy place indeed if the poor, bereaved and meek are blessed. Surely his listeners realized that Jesus' kingship is unlike any other that they had experienced. This is a long way from strategies to overthrow the Romans. This is unexpected. This is directed at the inside of every individual, not the outside. This is a spiritual kingdom.

Yet again, Jesus challenges our ideas. We long for strength and power. He tells us instead that it is in humility of spirit that we will find blessing. Only when we know that, of ourselves, we are spiritually bankrupt, will we discover the riches awaiting us in God's kingdom. When we are longing for God, hungrily, painfully, then we will find him. Only in real searching will he be found.

It may not actually feel very blessed at the time, to be thirsting for something or feeling empty of resources. Mourning doesn't sound much fun, but it is only when we are stripped of our pride, securities, daft ideas or grand schemes that we realize God is all we have and all we need. There is no better, or blessed, place to be.

Jesus did it all so differently. He had none of the trappings of power, no army, no protection, yet he was still a king and his kingdom has lasted longer than any other. We can trust him when he shares its values with us, don't you think?

'My kingdom,' said Jesus, 'doesn't consist of what you see around you… I'm not that kind of king, not the world's kind of king' (John 18:36, THE MESSAGE*).*

DA

The suffering king

From that time on Jesus began to explain to his disciples that he must go to Jerusalem and suffer many things at the hands of the elders, chief priests and teachers of the law, and that he must be killed and on the third day be raised to life. Peter took him aside and began to rebuke him. 'Never, Lord!' he said. 'This shall never happen to you!'

I was talking to someone the other day who said that she hated Easter Saturday. She found the day long and empty, every year. She spent Good Friday concentrating on the awful events of the crucifixion of Jesus and she just couldn't wait till Easter Sunday. I can remember as a child desperately wanting the Easter story to be different—perhaps this year Jesus would not have to die.

How gracious of Jesus to prepare his disciples for something that they didn't want to hear about either. How typical of many of us that Peter immediately tried to reject such terrible news. Why, Peter had seen all sorts of miracles and was no doubt full of excitement about the future. He must have wondered what on earth Jesus was talking about.

What does it mean to you that Jesus is a suffering king? It took me years to accept that there was no other way for Jesus. He took the hardest route, out of obedience and out of love for you and me. Unlike me, he faced suffering head on and even tried to help his friends to cope with it. Of course I am glad that he did, but we follow an extraordinary Lord. Part of his kingship was expressed in weakness and suffering. Do we find that reassuring or would we rather that our God was always big, strong and in control? What was happening to Jesus' kingship as he staggered to the cross? What difference does it make to the way we think of him and relate to him?

Jesus the King: obedient, compassionate, serving, suffering, receiving and totally unique. No wonder people reacted to him. What does his kingship mean in your life?

DA

Kingdom values

The kingdom of heaven is like treasure hidden in a field. When a man found it, he hid it again, and then in his joy went and sold all he had and bought that field.

Jesus is king, yet, as we have seen, he is like no other. Yes, he rode into Jerusalem on a donkey and accepted the adulation of the crowds, but otherwise he bursts out of stereotypes all the time. He does, however, talk a lot about his kingdom. Matthew's Gospel is littered with the phrase 'the kingdom of heaven'. It was one of Jesus' favourite topics. In the verse above, Jesus draws a picture for us of something so precious, it is worth all that we have. If Jesus' kingship breaks the mould, what about his kingdom?

Jesus makes it clear that the entrance ticket to his kingdom is repentance. Someone has said that the door to the kingdom of heaven is low—we can only get through it on our knees. As Christians, we need to remember this. We got in by grace and we live there by grace. We don't earn the right to stay—we are given it. There is nothing to prove. We are free to enjoy our treasure.

For a first-century Jew, the call to repentance must have been a shock. After all, the Jews were Abraham's descendents, God's chosen people. Surely they were already in? However, they too needed to own up to wrong thoughts and actions, just like us.

All who repent are welcomed with open arms. Then we learn more about our new kingdom. It is a precious place, like treasure, but also a challenging place. Having been forgiven our sins to enter, we are asked to forgive others—with no limits. This applies to friends and enemies. Surely one of the most famous sayings of Jesus is the command to love your enemies. I don't suppose that was any less startling then than it is now.

Read Matthew 6:14–15. How are those kingdom values of repentance and forgiveness at work in your life?

DA

Kingdom contradictions

'From the days of John the Baptist until now, the kingdom of heaven has been forcefully advancing, and forceful men lay hold of it.'

He told them another parable: 'The kingdom of heaven is like a mustard seed... Though it is the smallest of all your seeds, yet when it grows, it is the largest of garden plants and becomes a tree, so that the birds of the air come and perch in its branches.'

This kingdom of heaven can seem full of contradictions. On the one hand, Jesus tells us, it is forcefully advancing. On the other, it is growing secretly and quietly. As with the Beatitudes, whenever Jesus talks about his kingdom, he is likely to turn our thoughts inside out.

Like the two pedals on a bicycle, these apparent contradictions can work together. There is no doubt that, at times, advancing God's kingdom takes guts, determination and total commitment. Think of missionaries hauling their families to far-flung regions, leaving security behind. Think of organizations such as Tearfund, rushing to disaster zones and working for change all the time. Think of a mum at the school gate, inviting another mum to an Alpha course. All pretty forceful really.

Then again, the kingdom also grows quietly, producing fruit unexpectedly. I am thinking of the man who interrupted my husband gardening because he wanted to know how to become a Christian. He'd been reading about it.

Contradictions? Well, the kingdom of heaven is an open banquet—but you must come with the right clothes on. It is a precious pearl to be grasped, but you must give it away. You are always welcome, but the last shall be first. It will involve suffering, but is worth giving all for. It will give you the keys to heaven, but you must become like little children. It's only for the righteous, but you'll be surprised at who they are. It's here now, but not yet.

Dear Father, help me to learn more about what being in your kingdom means for me and to enjoy it!

DA

King over evil

The Pharisees... said, 'It is only by Beelzebub, the prince of demons, that this fellow drives out demons.' Jesus... said to them, 'Every kingdom divided against itself will be ruined... If Satan drives out Satan, he is divided against himself.'

Inevitably, Jesus' unique take on kingship attracts opposition as well as support. Most of the antagonism comes directly from the Jewish religious leaders of his day, who question what authority he has for both his teaching and actions. They cannot see who Jesus really is. Jesus takes them to task for their short-sightedness, calling them hypocrites, snakes and vipers (Matthew 23). Not very kingly language, you might think. Jesus must feel strongly about their inadequate spiritual leadership. Leading others is a fearsome thing.

Here, the Pharisees are accusing Jesus of being evil. Jesus has just healed a demon-possessed man who is blind and mute (v. 22) and the Pharisees have two options: Jesus is either using God's power or Satan's. Desperate to challenge Jesus' authority, the Pharisees plump for Satan. Jesus shows incredible restraint in pointing out to them their faulty logic. How can Satan drive himself out? He would fall to bits. Now the religious leaders are faced with the logical conclusion that Jesus is from God, but this is the bit they are trying to avoid.

Jesus challenges his accusers in turn: 'But if I drive out demons by the Spirit of God, then the kingdom of God has come upon you' (v. 28). Jesus proves his authority by his actions. Being able to drive out demons from people is a consequence of the choice he made back in the desert of temptation. He is on God's side and God has authority over evil. While the people around him struggle to accept Jesus as king, the spiritual realm has no hesitation. When demons meet Jesus, they flee. They know that they are no match for him. He is the king!

The controlled world of Western civilization says that demons don't exist. Jesus acts as if they do. Who is right? Read Ephesians 6:10–20.

DA

King Jesus

I saw… someone 'like a son of man', dressed in a robe reaching down to his feet and with a golden sash round his chest. His head and hair were white like wool, as white as snow, and his eyes were like blazing fire. His feet were like bronze glowing in a furnace, and his voice was like the sound of rushing waters. In his right hand he held seven stars, and out of his mouth came a sharp double-edged sword. His face was like the sun shining in all its brilliance.

I am sure that, like the first-century Jews, we all have days when it is hard to see Jesus as king. We are blinded by our circumstances or expectations. Our vision becomes clouded by our limited understanding, fears and doubts. Our Jesus is not big enough.

I hope that moving to Revelation for the last day that we consider the idea of Jesus as king will leave us with a challenge to meet with Jesus as he really is. Have another look at the passage above. Can you picture it? It feels to me as if John is struggling for words. This Jesus is huge! He is overwhelming! When John saw this vision of his friend, he fell down as if dead (v. 17)! John had known the earthly Jesus in all his captivating, confusing kingship but, in this vision, there is no doubt: John sees Jesus as king.

This king really is big enough. He is big enough to defeat evil. He is big enough to bring justice. He is big enough to wrap up the world at the end of time. He is big enough for your problems and mine. He does have the ultimate authority over everything. He is holy. He is the first and the last. What's more, he is coming back.

Jesus promises that he is going to return. When he does, we will not question his authority or identity. There won't be any doubt. Every knee will bow.

Read Revelation 22. Dear Jesus, help me to see you as you really are.

DA

Modern-day Job

'Have you not put a hedge around him and his household and everything he has? You have blessed the work of his hands, so that his flocks and herds are spread throughout the land.'

'On my 50th birthday,' sighed Sylvia, 'I realized that I had everything I ever wanted! We were heavily involved in a wonderful church; our kids were happy and doing well; Mike's business was thriving and God seemed to be blessing us lavishly in every direction. Then, in a remarkably short time, everything crashed round our ears! Our son was killed in a car accident; our daughter's husband left her; I was diagnosed with ME and the business nosedived—we lost everything, including our home.

'At first I felt so close to God, my friends said that I was a wonderful example of faith; but after a bit I began to think, "How could God treat us like this?" We'd both worked so hard for our church that our home was nicknamed the Church Hall because they used it so much. We prayed faithfully for our children, yet God hadn't taken care of them. All we ever tried to do was serve him so why had he dumped us?

'Of course all my friends knew exactly why! We were told we were harbouring secret sin; we'd left ourselves open to Satan's attack; God was punishing us or testing our faith. I felt utterly confused. The God I'd always loved and trusted had suddenly turned into a sadistic monster. When we talked about how we felt and asked questions, people at church said we were pity partying or being negative and bitter; their judgmental attitude made us feel that they had dumped us, too!'

Reading the book of Job was the one thing that really helped Sylvia. It did not answer her question 'Why do bad things happen to good people?' but it did encourage her to look at her experience through a wide-angle lens.

Please, Lord, help me to be as faithful as Job in praying for my family and friends.

JRL

Love hungry

'Did you notice my servant Job?' the Lord asked. 'There is no one on earth as faithful and good as he is. He worships me and is careful not to do anything evil. You persuaded me to let you attack him for no reason at all, but Job is still as faithful as ever.'

What a drama! God, beaming with pride and delight, almost says, 'I told you so', but his heart must have sunk when Satan produced his second cunning plan. When you really love someone, you can't bear to see them suffer, so letting Satan have another go at Job must have torn God apart! We know, from watching Jesus, that God minds so much when we hurt that he weeps for us (John 11:35). God also risks losing Job's friendship. Satan might have been right—perhaps Job didn't really love him, he just liked the prosperity and protection God gave him.

It is because God loves us so much that he yearns for us to return his love, yet some of us love the trappings of Christianity more than God himself. We treat him like an impersonal insurance policy rather than our most intimate companion. We go to church to see our friends, for exciting worship or a role that will make us feel needed and worth something. God could well feel like a multi-billionaire who has been married only for his money!

I don't think I could relate to a God who sat in heaven, thinking up horrible disasters to test my love for him, but I do believe that he wants to use the bad times that hit us all—eventually. They face us with the choice of turning away from God in disgust or moving nearer—clinging to him for support. I know when I've clung like that during my difficult experiences he has shown me such tenderness and personal care that my love for him has grown more rapidly than ever before.

It is hard to love an abstract spirit—that's why Jesus came to show us what God is really like.

JRL

Treasure hunt

Job went and sat by the rubbish heap and took a piece of broken pottery to scrape his sores. His wife said… 'Why don't you curse God and die?' Job answered, '… When God sends us something good, we welcome it. How can we complain when he sends us trouble?' Even in all this suffering Job said nothing against God.

Poor Mrs Job—she suffered the same set of horrendous losses as her husband, but how differently she reacted. In spite of all the rude things he says to God later in the book, Job never quite lets go of his faith, but she did and disappears from history. God gave us the gift of choice, but it must break his heart when we choose to reject him. Her decision must have hurt Job, too. Huddled in the local refuse tip, he must have felt utterly abandoned, without even his wife's support.

Have you ever felt as if your life has been chucked on the rubbish dump? I have—and it's a bleak experience. Right in the middle of a busy, fulfilling life, a brain virus left me facing permanent disability. At the time I remember thinking, 'I could have done so much for God if he hadn't dumped me in a wheelchair!' It was not until later that I realized God wasn't wasting my life, but wanted to enrich it enormously. His priority is not our comfort or prosperity, it is our faith, which Peter says is 'more precious than gold' (1 Peter 1:6–7).

Job had lived a trouble-free life, respected, successful and healthy. He was in control of his life and scarcely needed to rely on God at all. Actually, 'being in control' is only an illusion because human life is so fragile. God knows our only hope of security and happiness is to depend on him in every single area of our lives because of his infinitely superior power and knowledge. Health, success and prosperity increase our independence, but God wanted Job to have God-dependence—the most precious treasure of all.

Lord, increase my faith.

JRL

Pity party

After this, Job opened his mouth and cursed the day of his birth. He said... 'Why did I not perish at birth, and die as I came from the womb?'

Job behaved so well—at first. Perhaps he felt the numb, unreal feeling that often follows a severe shock? Then the shock hits him, he realizes just how much he has lost and grief sets in with a vengeance. He certainly sounds very sorry for himself, but who wouldn't be after such a ghastly experience? Pain like that needs to be talked out, but very few people are patient enough to listen without offering advice, looking shocked at our wild outbursts or trying to hurry us through our grief because it is making them feel uncomfortable! Real friends help most by listening quietly however many times we say the same thing! Job may well have been delighted to see his friends, he certainly needed them (6:14), but keeping quiet for that first week (2:13) was the only thing they ever did to help him!

The whole scenario would have been so much easier for Job if only he could have seen into heaven and realized what was really going on. Satan and God both wanted to use his situation—Satan to destroy him, God to bless him. God also wanted to help the many thousands of suffering people who would read about Job in the years to come. Job was not a mere pawn in some game God and Satan were playing but, rather, had the power to choose which of them won! Yet, he had no idea what a VIP he was, he just felt totally trashed, sitting there in the ashes. Blinded by misery, he couldn't see God watching him with such tender compassion as he urged him to go on trusting, just a little bit longer.

Lord, when I next face a difficult situation, make me aware that you and Satan both want to use it—you to bless me, Satan to harm me. Help me to give you the victory.

JRL

Worst fear

I have no peace, no quietness; I have no rest, but only turmoil.

Grief is a short word but it describes an enormous tangle of strong emotions, muddled thoughts, broken dreams and lost goalposts. We don't just experience grief after someone dies, it sets in after a relationship, marriage or friendship breaks up; when we lose our health, job, role or home. Grief always takes longer than we think it will and much longer than other people think it should!

Fear is usually part of the package, so Job's outburst in today's passage is no surprise. Fear shows up in many disguises, right from a paralysing panic attack that hits so suddenly in the supermarket that you think you're about to die, right down to a slowly churning cement mixer in the stomach. As human beings, we gain our sense of security from the people who matter to us, from our role, appearance and possessions. When one or, in Job's case, all of these things are yanked away, we are left feeling as vulnerable as a snail without a shell. For a long time after a major loss, many of us are plagued by lack of confidence. Facing people, going out alone, making decisions, even answering the phone can be terrifying.

Obviously Job had always had a secret dread (v. 25), but fear is not only the prerogative of the grieving—most people have a worst fear. What is yours? Perhaps you have never let yourself think about it before, but hidden fear can be very powerful. Facing it robs it of power. John tells us that 'in fear there is torment', but also that 'God is love' and 'perfect love drives out fear' (1 John 4:18). God used the thing that Job feared most to bless him hugely. If your fear should became a reality, God is able to do exactly the same for you.

Sit quietly and imagine your worst fear locked in a cupboard in a dark corner of your mind. Picture yourself opening that cupboard and allowing the light and love of Jesus to pour into it.

JRL

Reasons and causes

Who, being innocent, has ever perished?... those who plough evil and those who sow trouble reap it.

The news shocked us as we waited together at the school gate. One of us, the mother of a six-year-old, had died suddenly in the night. 'I told her she'd have a heart attack if she didn't lose weight,' said one (slim) mum with a hint of satisfaction. 'And she smoked, you know,' added another. 'Well, I think it was all that rushing about—she had three part-time jobs, you know.' Their reactions infuriated me, but I suppose we all feel safer if we know the cause of someone else's disaster so we can avoid it ourselves.

From babyhood we are taught the rule of cause and effect: 'If you touch the fire you'll be burnt'. Thus, we automatically look for a reason for everything. We forget that God never promises to make things fair in this life, only in the next.

Job understood that (19:25–27), but his friends—like many of us—believed in God's justice 'here and now', so it seemed logical that Job's misery was God's punishment for some secret sin that he was refusing to confess (4:7–8). Bildad even suggested that Job's children had died because they sinned (8:4)! That must have been a harsh one for poor Job, considering how faithfully he had prayed for them (1:4–5). Their advice was simple: repent and God will put everything right (5:8; 11:13–20). Job never pretended to be perfect, but he knew that he had never done anything to deserve such cruel punishment.

Condemning words are even more painful when they are prefaced by, 'The Lord told me to say that...'. Eliphaz did just that to Job (4:12–19). Perhaps it was not God's Spirit but Satan he saw (2 Corinthians 11:13)? When God gives us a message for someone else it is always encouraging, never destructive, nor judgmental.

Have you ever been on the receiving end of unfair, ill-informed criticism or phoney 'words from the Lord'? It's comforting to know how angry they make God (Job 42:7–8).

JRL

Switchback

Month after month I have nothing to live for;
night after night brings me grief...

No! I can't be quiet! I am angry and bitter.

One minute Job is furiously angry, the next he plunges into hopelessness and depression. If only he'd had a bereavement counsellor to explain that the grief journey feels like a switchback ride! One minute you can be almost happy again, then a song on the radio plunges you back into the depths.

Our unexpected anger can also astound and embarrass us. Even the calmest temperaments feel prickly while grieving; prone to bursts of rage at inappropriate moments, often directed at kind friends who only want to help. Their shocked expressions make us feel worse.

Job was angry with God and livid with his friends. Most of us are so afraid of anger that we hastily bury it, but pushing it down can actually cause physical, emotional and spiritual problems later on. Some kind of vigorous exercise or DIY are my preferred methods of expending anger, but Job was too ill for anything like that (7:5), so he used words.

However, he was unwise to direct them at those who had hurt him—it only made them fight back. Even when you are in the right, it is better to follow the example of Jesus who never said a word to the people who were treating him so unfairly (1 Peter 2:19–23), but he did express his pain to his Father (Matthew 27:46). God is big enough to take all our anger—he let Job verbally punch and kick him for a surprisingly long time—yet we must always remember that, because he loves us so much, we are able to hurt God badly if we keep on misjudging and doubting him for too long, as Job did (38:1–2).

When one of my sons was angry with me he exploded, but his rage soon finished with a hug and a 'sorry'. His brother, however, would refuse to speak for days, which hurt me far more! Perhaps God feels the same?

JRL

The black hole

Even if I summoned him and he responded, I do not believe he would give me a hearing. He would crush me with a storm and multiply my wounds for no reason.

Shock froze our house-group into silence. Our good Christian smiles fell off as our mouths opened in surprise. Our leader, a church elder, was pouring out his pain in a far from positive tirade. His daughter was terminally ill, he had lost his job and his home was about to be repossessed. 'Either God's not powerful enough to help me or he's so cruel he just doesn't care!'

His finale unleashed a cloud of reproachful platitudes on his unrepentant head, but questions and doubts about previously long-held beliefs are yet another part of grief. When your faith in God's cast-iron goodness has been a central part of your life, the sudden loss of that faith feels horrendous. The sense of having lost God can be as painful as your initial bereavement.

I've christened this stage of grief 'the black hole'. My friend Mary went into it soon after losing her baby to cot death: 'I knew God existed, but I couldn't talk or even think about him because all my questions got in the way. I just couldn't believe he loved me, but I knew I was totally lost if he didn't! There was nowhere else to run. In the end I knew I just had to take his word for it, so I wrote out verses about his love and stuck them all over the place. I just had to keep on choosing to believe them by sheer willpower until my feelings and faith came back to life.'

Job did not doubt God's power (vv. 4–8), only his goodness (vv. 17–18, 23). Once again, we must remember that it was harder for Job than it is for us because Jesus had not yet shown humanity what God is really like. Even so, Job gives us remarkable prophetic pictures of Jesus (vv. 32–35; 16:19–21).

Lord, help me to doubt my doubts.

JRL

Hope

At least there is hope for a tree: if it is cut down, it will sprout again, and its new shoots will not fail. Its roots may grow old in the ground and its stump die in the soil, yet at the scent of water it will bud and put forth shoots like a plant.

The sermon was dull and I was in too much pain to sit still in my wheelchair, so, to pass the dragging time, I was flipping backwards through the book of Job. 'My spirit is broken... My days have passed, my plans are shattered, and so are the desires of my heart' (17:1, 11). 'Yes!' I thought, 'that's exactly how I feel!' As the brain virus had destroyed so much of my life, I felt, like Job, that I would never be happy or useful ever again.

Then, suddenly, the words, 'there is hope' (14:7) seemed to jump right out at me. At first glance I didn't realize Job was saying, 'Fallen trees have a hope of sprouting again but people don't get a second chance when they fall flat!' God just pulled the verse out of context to bless me and I remembered, as a child, making houses with my brother in an old apple tree. We loved that tree, but its apples tasted terrible. How we cried when a storm felled our tree, but out of the stump a new tree grew and its apples tasted wonderful. In church that night, my life felt like a fallen tree, fit only for firewood or the compost heap, but God reassured me that I was not finished—he really did have a new life waiting for me at the end of my grief journey.

Job seems to have little hope of anything good in this life and in his day people only had a very hazy concept of eternity because Jesus had not yet come to tell us about heaven. Yet Job doggedly holds on to the conviction he shared with Abraham (Genesis 18:25) that God will make things fair one day.

JRL

Passed with distinction!

Oh, that my words were recorded, that they were written on a scroll, that they were inscribed with an iron tool on lead, or engraved in rock forever!

'Thirty-one years!' sobbed Phoebe. 'He was the kindest husband in the world, my best friend! Then, suddenly, just because he fancies her, he starts treating me like dirt—turned into a monster overnight!'

When someone you don't particularly like walks out of your life you hardly notice the loss, but if you have loved and trusted a person most of your life, it hurts like crazy! Job moaned about all his many afflictions, but the thing he minded most was the loss of intimacy with God: 'You gave me life and showed me kindness, and in your providence watched over my spirit' (10:12). 'I have treasured the words of his mouth more than my daily bread' (23:12). His closest, life-long friend was not only treating him cruelly, but ignoring him without explanation (19:7; 13:23). Could Job's extreme reaction to God's lengthy silence actually be the reason for his proving to Satan that he loved God above everything else? If Job had not loved God deeply, he would not have been in such distress.

All down the centuries, God's friends have experienced the pain of his occasional, unexplained periods of absence. The mystics christened them 'the dark night of the soul'. That lovely feeling of being close to God, the buzz when prayers are answered and the joy of hearing him speak through his word, the mystics called 'consolations'. When God withdrew them, leaving you to pursue him with nothing but dogged faith, they felt it was a mark of maturity and not, as we often think, a sign of failure.

Satan had also insulted God by suggesting that he had to buy his friends with bribes and gifts, so God must have been delighted to grant Job's wish (19:23–24) in order to encourage countless others.

If you suddenly discovered that God was just a myth, what difference would it make to your life?

JRL

Candles in the dark

I know that my Redeemer lives, and that in the end he will stand upon the earth. And after my skin has been destroyed, yet in my flesh I will see God; I myself will see him with my own eyes— I, and not another. How my heart yearns within me!

These verses explode into the gloomy narrative like fireworks on a dark night! By this stage of the book, most of us are sick of Job! However did he get his reputation for patience? He goes round in despairing circles, repeating himself endlessly, arguing abusively with his friends and rudely shaking a verbal fist at God. Yet, now and then, he seems to have a tiny glimpse of what is really happening above the clouds of confusion and produces one of the little phrases that have formed candles in the dark for so many of us ever since.

He proved his love for God to Satan, but in verses 25–26 he proves his trust as well. In spite of all the accusations his friends hurled at him, he knew in his heart that God was on his side (v. 29). He expresses it again: 'Though he slay me, yet will I hope in him' (13:15) and we all know his statement about the crucible of suffering: 'When he has tried me, I will come forth as refined gold' (23:10, Amplified).

When I had to break the awful news that my father had suddenly died, my mother responded, as thousands of others have done, by using Job's first candle—'The Lord gave, and the Lord has taken away; blessed be the name of the Lord' (1:21, NKJV).

When God sends us something good, we welcome it. How can we complain when he sends us trouble (2:10)? I wonder if Job regretted that glib remark he made to his unfortunate wife right at the beginning of the book? He certainly didn't practise what he preached, but these candles prove that his wobbly faith was never completely destroyed.

Thank you for never leaving us in total darkness.

JRL

Spider's web

If you return to the Almighty, you will be restored… assign your nuggets to the dust, your gold of Ophir to the rocks in the ravines, then the Almighty will be your gold, the choicest silver for you. Surely then you will find delight in the Almighty and will lift up your face to God.

It would be wrong to dismiss Job's friends as baddies and devalue all they said—much of it is wise and beautiful. They just could not see past their rigid belief that bad things never happen to good people. In order to make him fit into their theology, they seem to have forgotten what the real Job is like (1:1). In his first speech, Eliphaz correctly describes his reputation (4:3–4), then says the exact opposite (vv. 5–9)! They all seem to be ganging up on Job to blacken his character.

When a chicken is ill, all the other hens cluster round and peck it to death. We do the same. Could you ever have been guilty of joining others to gossip unkindly or even untruthfully about another Christian who is going through a crisis of faith?

Perhaps Eliphaz shared Satan's opinion that Job's vast wealth had given him such a sense of security that he felt he did not need to depend on God for anything (22:24–25). Jesus told us how futile it is to depend on earthly wealth (Matthew 6:19–21). Some of us only feel safe when we have plenty of financial resources; others could live on air so long as they had a Mr Right to love and care for them. Our homes, children, career, health, even our Christian ministry, can become the thing that we rely on to make us feel good, safe and worth something. Eliphaz thought one of these props had taken God's place in Job's life and Bildad told him that people who trust something other than God for their security are in as much danger as someone who leans for support on a fragile spider's web (8:13–15).

What do you think is your spider's web?

JRL

Awesome interview

Will the one who contends with the Almighty correct him? Let him who accuses God answer him!' Then Job answered the Lord: 'I am unworthy—how can I reply to you? I put my hand over my mouth.'

Poor Job! He had been demanding this one to one with God for months but, when his big moment came, he couldn't say a word! Most of us have tough questions we want to fire at God when we meet him face to face, but we'll probably be as overawed as Job!

Nowhere, in his magnificent speech, does God once answer any of Job's questions. He doesn't offer many solutions to the problem of suffering anywhere else in the Bible either. Perhaps he knows our human minds simply are not large enough to cope. We can never hope to reach God via the rickety ladders of our intellect, only by a leap of faith. God merely says to Job, and to the rest of us, 'If you once realized how powerful, all-knowing and all-seeing I am, you would forget all your fussy little questions and simply trust my firm intention to make everything that ever happens to you work for your maximum benefit' (Romans 8:28). All you need to do is trust in him.

Reading chapters 38—41 of Job, we hear God, the creator, revelling in his universe. He talks about animals and birds no human had seen at that time. No camera crews had been sent into the deserts, oceans or mountains that were their habitats to make TV documentaries, yet God even knew the due date of each mountain goat (39:1). He admired the courage of a horse (39:19), laughed at the stupidity of an ostrich (39:13–18) and helped the lioness stalk her prey (38:39). He also knows how many hairs grow on your head (Matthew 10:30) and what you are about to say next (Psalm 139:4).

This is the awesome God who yearns for your personal love and friendship so much that he gave his life to win it!

JRL

Grand finale

After Job had prayed for his friends, the Lord made him prosperous again and gave him twice as much as he had before.

When you are trudging through a grief journey, you feel as if the real you has died; living no longer interests you. Then, suddenly, there comes a moment when happiness takes you by surprise. Often your outside circumstances have not changed, as Job's did, but you realize that you are coming alive again on the inside.

When Job remembered the rude things that he had said to God, he cringed, but when he repented God totally forgave and forgot. He only remembered the good things Job had said. Doubting God's goodness and ability to care for all our needs is actually the sin that hurts God most. Doubts are natural during grief, but they are still a sin we need to confess and renounce.

God was angry with Job's friends, but it was not until Job had diverted God's anger by forgiving and praying for them that his restoration began. During a grief journey, uncaring professionals, tactless friends or relatives and unsupportive pastors can easily hurt us. We never completely emerge from our grief until we are willing to forgive each one of them. Don't let grudges rob you of all the good things God wants to pour on you now.

By the end of his grief journey, Job, like many others, realized that his relationship with God had grown much deeper. To Satan this must have been the last straw! Not only had he been proved wrong, but he had also actually pushed Job closer to God—the very last thing he wanted. Job even seems to have married again because surely poor old Mrs Job could not have had ten more children after all she'd been through!

Having recently lost a granddaughter, I found verse 13 very comforting. God doubled everything Job had lost but gave him the same number of children—because the first ten were still alive, just waiting for him round the corner.

JRL

Unity in baptism

Peter replied, 'Repent and be baptized, every one of you, in the name of Jesus Christ for the forgiveness of your sins. And you will receive the gift of the Holy Spirit.'

For the next few weeks we will be looking at issues of unity—a concept that often seems more like an impossible dream than a genuine reality. What types of unity should Christians be aiming for? What difference does it, or could it, make in our lives? What does 'unity' mean anyway?

A good place to start is with baptism—the single initiation rite needed to become a member of the Christian Church. Baptism symbolizes dying to our old life and being born again in the new life of the Spirit. The water of baptism is where we are cleansed from our past and by means of which we are filled with a new well of life that will never run dry. In these symbolic actions we are united to Christ's dying and rising again.

As the apostle Paul said, 'We were therefore buried with him through baptism into death in order that, just as Christ was raised from the dead through the glory of the Father, we too may live a new life. If we have been united with him like this in his death, we will certainly also be united with him in his resurrection' (Romans 6:4–5). If you are not yet baptized, talk to someone who can help you to take this important step of faith.

Jesus himself was baptized by John in the Jordan river, even though John was acutely aware that his baptism with water was different from the baptism that Jesus would bring—with the Holy Spirit baptism. You can read Matthew's account of Jesus' baptism in Matthew 3.

Dear Lord, fill me afresh with your Holy Spirit, and wash me clean with your love. Help me to be full to overflowing with your love and light, so that people around me may be touched by your Holy Spirit.

CR

Unity in the Spirit

There are different kinds of gifts, but the same Spirit. There are different kinds of service, but the same Lord. There are different kinds of working, but the same God works all of them in all men.

Time and time again, Paul stresses the unity shared by those who believe in Jesus Christ. In this letter to the young church in Corinth, Paul emphasizes the unity that we have in the Holy Spirit. He teaches that all the various spiritual gifts that Christians are given come from the one Spirit and are given for the common good (v. 7). Paul lists nine gifts in this passage that he says are 'activated' by God and allotted to individuals as the Spirit chooses: wisdom, knowledge, faith, healing, miracles, prophecy, discernment of spirits, tongues and interpretation of tongues.

The picture is of God bestowing gifts on his children in order that believers can carry out the work of Christ. It is a huge pity that these gifts of the Spirit, intended to empower and equip Christians, have been used to create divisions in the Church. Some believers accept all the gifts listed by Paul as God-given and available to us now. Others argue that most of the gifts were meant only for New Testament times, to help the emerging Church get established. Some even believe that certain gifts, such as tongues, make them more 'spiritual' than those who have been given other gifts.

My own understanding and experience has convinced me that God has never stopped giving his beloved children gifts and all God's gifts are good. If we trust God, the giver, then we can open ourselves in confidence and expectation to receiving whichever gifts the Spirit chooses to give us, while also honouring and rejoicing in the gifts others have been given.

Generous Lord, thank you for your gifts that you long to give us. Help us to trust that all your gifts are good and, if we accept what you give us, we can be used to strengthen, build and unify your Church.

CR

Unity in the body

The body is a unit, though it is made up of many parts; and though all its parts are many, they form one body. So it is with Christ. For we were all baptized by one Spirit into one body—whether Jews or Greeks, slave or free—and we were all given the one Spirit to drink. Now the body is not made up of one part but of many.

Ancient and contemporary spirituality—and, indeed, our growing understanding of ecology—teaches the interconnectedness of all living things. How we live our lives affects the lives of people and other forms of life on the other side of the globe. There is no room for a concept of isolated action—we are all in this experience of life together.

In a very graphic, almost humorous way, Paul describes the special interconnectedness of those who are in Christ. The image he uses is that of a body in which all the individual parts work together for the good of the whole. He is trying to counteract the all too human tendency to give greater value to certain people who occupy certain positions or who perform certain roles in the Church by presenting imaginary conversations of various body parts: 'If the foot should say, "Because I am not a hand, I do not belong to the body", it would not for that reason cease to be part of the body' (v. 15).

The main point Paul is making is that no one person should be seen as being of unique importance or considered to outrank or do away with the need for any of the others. A body needs all its parts if it is to function in a healthy and effective manner. In this way, Paul is justifying diversity and speaking out against hierarchical ideas of value or importance.

Dear Lord, help us to see ourselves as you see us—precious and of great value—and help us to know that we are vital parts of the body of Christ.

CR

Unity in the faith

... so that the body of Christ may be built up until we all reach unity in the faith and in the knowledge of the Son of God and become mature, attaining to the whole measure of the fullness of Christ.

This passage in Ephesians builds on the image of the body used in 1 Corinthians 12:12, but points to a special goal for that body—maturity. In his letter to the Corinthians, Paul celebrated diversity in the body and warned against a hierarchical view of people and gifts. We should all be encouraged to use our gifts for the common good and everyone should be valued.

In Ephesians, this concept is expanded as it is explained that all the various gifts and roles, such as teachers, prophets and evangelists (v. 12), are needed if the body is to attain maturity in a corporate sense. This type of maturity is only possible for the body as a whole; it is not a maturity that can be experienced or expressed by the individuals that make up the body on their own. It is, of course, important that individuals are mature in their relationships and how they exercise their spiritual gifts, but the focus is on the Church—the body—as a whole. What is being hinted at here is the body working so well as one that it is able to reach a greater fullness in Christ, a fullness that results in yet further growth, with an overall increase of love.

This view of the Christian Church has no room for individual personal and spiritual growth that is not also connected to and used in the service of the wider Christian community. The grace that is given to us as individuals (Ephesians 4:7) may well bless us and equip us as individuals, but we are called to offer all that we are and all that we have been given to the building up of the body of Christ.

Lord of love, please help us to catch a glimpse of the vision of our wholeness in you.

CR

Unity in the living water

Jesus answered, 'Everyone who drinks this water will be thirsty again, but whoever drinks the water I give him will never thirst. Indeed, the water I give him will become in him a spring of water welling up to eternal life.'

Over and over again in the Gospels—most notably the John's—Jesus tries to explain the dynamic of the relationship he wants people to have with him. He uses simple, everyday, down-to-earth images of what he is attempting to convey. Here, Jesus encounters a woman at a well. She is from Samaria and would not have been of Jewish faith. By asking the woman for a drink, Jesus is breaking away from expected behaviour. First, he is a Jew speaking to a Samaritan and, second, he is a man speaking to a woman.

The woman expresses her astonishment by asking Jesus how he can make such a request, knowing that Jews do not associate with Samaritans. It is then that Jesus reveals to her the gift he is offering—water that quenches all thirst for those who drink it and that becomes a spring gushing up to eternal life.

The gift that Jesus is offering to the woman is a gift that God is still offering to everyone who follows Christ today. Those who accept this gift now have the living water in themselves; they have become part of the gushing spring. It can help to think of ourselves as being joined to others in Christ because of our acceptance of the living water. Our faith in God is not a dry or static thing, but an overflowing, dynamic relationship in which all who believe are sustained and refreshed in God's never-ending love.

Dear living Lord, when I am feeling thirsty and parched, show me how to draw from the spring of living water that is now in me as a gift of God. Let your life flow through me, transforming every part of my life and bringing life to others as I become a channel of your love and life.

CR

Unity in the bread of life

'I am the living bread that came down from heaven. If anyone eats of this bread, he will live forever.'

In this passage, Jesus is teaching his disciples about what it really means to do the work of God and about how the disciples are to view Jesus. Jesus tells them that the only way they can do the work of God is to believe in the one whom God has sent—that is, in Jesus himself. The disciples then ask for a sign so that they can be sure that Jesus really is the one whom God has sent. They remind Jesus that God sent manna from heaven when Moses asked for food. Jesus tells them that the bread that God sends is the true bread that 'gives life to the world' (v. 33). It is not bread in a physical sense, but in a spiritual sense. When the disciples ask for this special type of bread, Jesus declares that he himself is the bread of life.

The people are eager to discover exactly what it is that will please God, but they do not understand what Jesus is trying to communicate. They are not meant to dash about trying to do things for God, but, rather, are to let God accomplish what he wants to do through them. They please God by their response of faith in Jesus himself. The best 'work' that they can do is to believe in Jesus, then live in the way he shows and teaches them.

This passage spells freedom from striving for those who follow Christ. We are to 'feed' on Jesus in our hearts, rely on him to sustain and nourish us, then trust that he will show us how we are to live. Of course, there will be work to do for God, but it will be work borne out of a faith in the one who lives in us and continually feeds us from within.

Lord, please help us to understand how we are meant to feed on you.

CR

Unity in the true light

In him was life, and that life was the light of men.

When we are in complete darkness, it is impossible to see. Also, when we don't know what to do, we sometimes say that we are 'in the dark'. John begins his account of Jesus' life and teachings by describing Jesus as the light that 'shines in the darkness' (v. 5) and as the 'true light that gives light to every man' (v. 9).

This image of Jesus is a strong one of a light being lit in the middle of pitch darkness, and John is implying that the coming of Jesus will transform our lives and our world as much as a light transforms a dark room. John's message is that Jesus will show us the truth about ourselves and God and that believing in Jesus will be the spiritual equivalent of switching on a light in an otherwise dark place.

If we turn to Matthew's Gospel, to the Sermon on the Mount, we read something startling that Jesus said to his followers: 'You are the light of the world.' John declared that the light was in Jesus, yet here, Jesus himself is telling his disciples that they are the light. So, who's right—John or Jesus?

The answer is that both are correct as Jesus is the light and everyone who has faith in Jesus becomes filled with the light of Christ. What an awesome thought! Our faith in Jesus Christ makes us a light in the darkness. Christians bring the light of Christ into the world.

What am I doing with my light? Am I living in such a way that the light of Christ can shine clearly out from me? Do I speak words of truth, life and hope to people or am I covering up my light and stumbling around in the dark?

Dear Lord of truth, help me to trust that, by faith in you, I, too, have your loving and life-transforming light shining in me. May my life inspire other people to trust in you.

Read Matthew 5:14–16.

CR

Unity in the vine

'I am the vine; you are the branches. If a man remains in me and I in him, he will bear much fruit; apart from me you can do nothing.'

One of my favourite images of our unity in Christ is the image of the vine. I can picture a beautiful, sun-drenched vineyard with the vine's branches curling and twining around the supporting stakes and wires. In among the green and golden leaves hang large bunches of sweet and succulent grapes, ripe for the picking.

As with the images of water, bread and light, this is yet another striking image that Jesus uses to describe his relationship with us and his Father. It speaks of great intimacy, love and joy.

One of the key words in this passage is 'abide', with its connotations of rest, trust and lack of striving. To abide is to exist without anxiety, to grow and flourish in an atmosphere of intimate trust and nurture. It is only from within this relationship of abiding that we are able to produce fruit.

Another important theme is love. A little earlier, Jesus taught his disciples his new commandment: love one another as I have loved you (John 13:34). Over and over again, Jesus stresses the need for this love, which he ties into the act of abiding. We are to abide in Jesus' love for us and our love for one another.

Closely related to the intimacy and love is the concept of joy. Jesus' friends are not to be distinguished by their worried, care-worn or dreary expressions, but by a joy that is similar to the joy Jesus himself experiences in his relationship with his Father. Jesus actually wants us to share in his own experience of joy.

Do we really believe that this is what Jesus wants for us? Do we dare to abide and let go of our anxious striving? Will we risk loving others and allowing Jesus' joy to flow though our veins? What will our lives be like if we don't do these things?

CR

Jesus' prayer for unity

'May they also be in us so that the world may believe that you have sent me. I have given them the glory that you gave me, that they may be one as we are one: I in them and you in me. May they be brought to complete unity.'

If you want to find out whether or not Jesus really intended his followers to be united, then look no further than chapter 17 in John's Gospel! The entire chapter contains Jesus' final prayer before he allowed himself to be arrested in the Garden of Gethsemane. It reveals the deep and trusting intimacy he shared with his Father. The amazing and humbling thing for us is that Jesus shows that he wants to have that same type of intimacy with us as well.

Part of the prayer is for the friends he will soon be leaving, but in verse 20 Jesus widens the scope to include 'those who will believe in me' because of the disciples' ministry. That's us! Indeed, everyone who believes in Jesus and didn't meet him while he lived on earth is included in the remaining words of the prayer.

As Jesus pours his heart out to his Father, we hear how fervently he longs for unity among his disciples and unity for all future believers. Part of the reason Jesus prays for our unity is so that, when people meet us, they will see evidence that Jesus was indeed sent by God and that we are as loved by God as Jesus was.

In the light of this prayer, perhaps we would bring more joy to God if we were to emphasize our faith in the death and resurrection of Jesus Christ and stand alongside one another in solidarity about that. Perhaps then we could lean more lightly on those things about which we disagree.

Dear God of all wisdom, please help us to keep our eyes on Jesus. Forgive us for all our divisions and lead us deeper into your truth and love.

CR

Unity in suffering

The Spirit himself testifies with our spirit that we are God's children. Now if we are children, then we are heirs—heirs of God and co-heirs with Christ, if indeed we share in his sufferings in order that we may also share in his glory.

Being alive on planet earth is a mixed bag. Alongside exquisite beauty and immense joy, we also experience much grief and anguish. Suffering is part of our reality, and no one can escape it.

Christians have a peculiar relationship with suffering. We believe that, despite all the evidence to the contrary, God is a loving God who ultimately has everything under control. Our destiny in Christ is a joyous, loving eternal existence in the very heart of God, but until then, as Paul puts it 'the whole creation has been groaning as in the pains of childbirth right up to the present time' (v. 22). Not only individuals, but the entire created world experiences the effects of separation from God, with all its painful consequences.

Our hope is in the power of God that was able to raise Jesus from the dead and in the Spirit who lives in us and helps us to endure whatever life brings our way. Paul is such a realist—he recognizes that some of the time we don't even know how to pray! Although Paul insists that sin has been overcome, its tragic legacy remains. True discipleship is costly and suffering is an inevitable part of the experience of following Jesus Christ.

The good news is that, thanks to Jesus, we can count on God's unending and unfailing love. It is this love that turns out to be the greatest power in the universe. No amount of suffering, no experience, however dreadful, is able to separate us from God's love.

Dear Lord, when I suffer, help me to remember that I am not alone. Everyone else also suffers in some way and your love is with us and able to make us 'conquerors'.

CR

Unity in the cross

Now if we died with Christ, we believe that we will also live with him.

The cross, that ancient implement of torture and death, has become the universal symbol of the Christian faith. It might seem odd that a faith declaring the boundless love of a living God should have as its emblem the object on which Jesus was put to death.

We are taught that Jesus died on the cross for the sins of the world—yours, mine and every person's who has ever, or will ever, live. The cross stands as God's final pronouncement on sin, evil, sorrow and death. The last words that Jesus spoke from the cross as recorded by John are, 'It is finished.'

As followers of Christ, we will suffer. Many Christians are still dying for their faith, but no one has to save the world; that's what Jesus accomplished. We don't fully understand what the cross means—we never can. The cross unites those who follow Christ in a way that is impossible to explain adequately in words: our true and deepest response will spring from our hearts and will only be known fully by our Lord.

The well-known hymn by Isaac Watts puts it about as well as it can be expressed:

When I survey the wondrous cross
On which the Prince of glory died,
My richest gain I count but loss,
And pour contempt on all my pride.

Forbid it, Lord, that I should boast
Save in the death of Christ my God;
All the vain things that charm me most,
I sacrifice them to his Blood.

See from his head, his hands, his feet,
Sorrow and love flow mingled down;
Did e'er such love and sorrow meet,
Or thorns compose so rich a crown?

Were the whole realm of nature mine,
That were a present far too small;
Love so amazing, so divine,
Demands my soul, my life, my all.

ISAAC WATTS (1674–1748)

CR

Unity in the resurrection

For as in Adam all die, so in Christ all will be made alive.

For Paul, the reality of the resurrection was crucial and so he spends much of chapter 15 of his first letter to the Corinthians explaining the centrality of the risen Christ. It appears that some of the believers in Corinth were doubting aspects of the resurrection. Paul counteracts these doubts with his assertion regarding the significance of the risen Lord.

His argument runs almost like a legal document, with lots of 'if… then' clauses, the last of these stating that if Christ was not raised, then of all people, Christians are to be the most pitied. However, he claims, Jesus was raised from the dead and, with him, we too can have confidence in having new life in Christ.

Sometimes the phrase 'we walk by faith, not by sight' can fall rather glibly from our lips, but our faith is truly tested when we consider the resurrection. What do I believe happened to the body of Jesus? If I believe he was raised from the dead, what can I know about his new life? What does it mean for me?

Along with many other Christians, I believe that Jesus was resurrected into a genuinely new type of life and that his body wasn't merely resuscitated on that first Easter morning. I believe that Jesus was both still himself and something else—he had become the Christ more fully since his crucifixion. Like the crucifixion, we cannot know for certain exactly what took place—what was transacted spiritually and eternally—but we are assured that we, too, are made alive in a new way because of Christ's resurrection. As Paul writes elsewhere, 'And if the Spirit of him who raised Jesus from the dead is living in you, he who raised Christ from the dead will also give life to your mortal bodies through his Spirit, who lives in you' (Romans 8:11).

Dear God, thank you for giving us your Spirit, which gives us new life in Christ.

CR

Unity in the love of God

Dear friends, since God so loved us, we also ought to love one another. No one has ever seen God; but if we love one another, God lives in us and his love is made complete in us.

Jesus' beloved friend John is now an old man. He is living on Patmos, that jewel of an island in the Aegean Sea, writing, thinking, praying and remembering the three years he spent with Jesus and his other friends. He is still driven to communicate what he has learned and pass on the wisdom he has gained.

One of his most important insights is to convey the primacy of God's love for us. It was God who first loved us, who sent Jesus to show us what God is like, and it is up to us how we respond to that love. Closely allied to the love of God is our love for one another. If we know ourselves to be loved by God, then we will naturally be moved to share that love with others.

When John writes 'God is love' (v. 16), he is not being vague or mystical, he is describing how he experiences God. The one who is loved by God will return that love to God and will also show that love to fellow believers. In fact, the prime characteristic of a Christian will be this love.

To receive God's love and share it with others remains the Christian goal, purpose and meaning: there is nothing higher to aim for. Nothing surpasses the love of God and nothing more accurate can be said about God than that 'God is love'. In this passage, John again uses the word 'abide'—a word he emphasized when he wrote of the image of the vine in his Gospel. This is, in a sense, a summation of his understanding of who God is and of how we are to live, which can be even more succinctly and clearly summed up by the word 'love'.

Dear Lord, enfold us in your love so that we may be the living expression of your love on earth.

CR

Claiming our unity

Therefore, if anyone is in Christ, he is a new creation; the old has gone, the new has come!

We can do much to further the cause of unity by claiming our unity! If we believe that Jesus desires that we are united in God's love, and if we believe that unity is our ultimate goal, then why don't we start living it now?

Of course, that's easier said than done—it's hard enough to have a unified family, much less a unified Church and much less a unified Christendom! That's our goal, though, that's where we're heading and we can bring it about more surely if we refuse to let the things that divide us get in the way of the things that unite us.

It also helps to remember that Paul believed that God has given us the ministry of reconciliation—the work of reuniting the world with God through Christ. So, how do we begin? First, we can accept that God loves us all and that God has no favourites—much as we might secretly wish was the case! Second, we can pray for those with whom we disagree or from whom we are estranged. Third, we can treat all people with respect and, fourth, we can try to live our lives with as much honesty and integrity as we can, and trust God with the consequences. I realize that, just by being who I am and speaking honestly about what I believe, I may alienate and divide some people, but I believe that God's eternal truth, justice and love will prevail.

This is not an easy walk, but it is the one to which we are called. However, we are not to do it using our own strength alone. God's Holy Spirit—the same Spirit who was able to raise Jesus from the dead—lives in us. Perhaps the greatest step towards unity that we can take is to allow the Spirit to refresh us continually and abide in God's love.

Remember, if we abide in God's love we will bear much fruit.

CR

God's cosmic plan

In the past God spoke to our forefathers through the prophets... but in these last days he has spoken to us by his Son... The Son is the radiance of God's glory and the exact representation of his being.

However much it may seem like it, our world is not hurtling along in ever-increasing chaos. God has a plan and he is steadily and inexorably bringing it to fruition.

This letter to the Hebrews draws on Jewish history to show God's long-term planning. The events mentioned would have been familiar to the original readers of this letter. Abraham and Moses were household names in Jewish homes, but now these readers needed to move on and embrace the next stage in the unfolding of God's plan.

The writer reminds them that God had communicated with his people in the past through prophets, but now he had sent his Son, Jesus—not a messenger of God, but God himself: 'the exact representation of his being'. This startling news was difficult for them to take in. They thought of God as holy and set apart, not able to be approached or touched for fear of death. To think of God as a flesh and blood man, walking and talking in their grimy world, stretched their imagination to the utmost.

Old Testament scriptures are used to emphasize repeatedly that Jesus is greater than any prophet. He is greater even than angels, and they are scary enough. Jesus is on a completely different plane. A new kind of relationship with God is born.

God illuminates his cosmic plan in this letter. There is a throne in heaven and it is not vacant (Revelation 4:2). What a relief to know that someone is in charge not only of world events, but also our individual destinies. Despite terrorist bombs, world and family conflict fuelled by hatred and anger, God will not be deflected from his purpose to reach out in love and mercy to wayward people.

Read Hebrews 4:16 and approach him with confidence.

CP

God's recovery plan

What is man that you are mindful of him, the son of man that you care for him? You made him a little lower than the angels; you crowned him with glory and honour and put everything under his feet.

This was God's original blueprint for life on earth—men and women, glorious, honourable, having mastery over everything. This quotation comes from Psalm 8, which sings of the glory of humanity.

As we know, this god-like image became deeply marred. We are not what we ought to be. Many of us don't live up to the meagre standards we set ourselves, let alone God's. The fantastic truth, though, is that God has not abandoned his original purpose. He has not lowered his high calling for men and women. Instead, he dealt a body blow to the enemy who brought about our catastrophic fall (v. 14). By his death, Jesus, the flesh and blood man, made it possible for us to be restored to glory and honour. He heals and brings wholeness to our fractured souls.

I distinctly remember the mind-shattering moment when I grasped that my real self was holy, good, perfect, full of beauty and truth. I'd grown accustomed to living a substandard Christian life and believed my true identity was weak, selfish and impatient. I kept trying to change and become someone other than my real self. It was incredibly liberating to realize that I just needed to cooperate with God as he worked on restoring the original person he'd made me to be.

It's like having a dirty, marked wooden table. However much you clean it and polish it, if the original wood is rotten, it will never look good. However, if the wood underneath is sound, all you have to do is strip the muck and rubbish off and let its original beauty come out. God is the master of restoration.

Lord, I praise you that you see me as a beautiful person. Please restore me to be the person you made me to be.

CP

Ultimate rescue package

Holy brothers, who share in the heavenly calling, fix your thoughts on Jesus... Jesus has been found worthy of greater honour than Moses.

When the Jewish converts read this letter they would have been shocked out of their socks by verse 3. Moses was the specially chosen servant to whom God revealed his law (Exodus 20) and to whom God spoke face to face (Exodus 33:11). The law was as vital to them as breath.

The writer has already shown that Jesus was greater than angels (Hebrews 1:4). Now he claims that Jesus is superior to Moses. Whereas Moses was God's servant, Jesus is God's Son (Hebrews 3:5–6). This is not to undermine the significance of Moses' life as his walk of faith is a graphic prefiguration of what Jesus accomplished. Moses led the people of God out of slavery in Egypt to the promised land. Jesus rescues people from the slavery of sin and brings them into freedom (2:14).

How can we walk in that freedom? Try putting your own name in verse 1. Therefore, Jane, you are a holy person who has been invited by God himself to know him here on earth and to be with him forever in heaven. Stay focused on Jesus.

We need to claim our identity as holy people, chosen by God, and keep our eyes on our Saviour.

When Peter got out of the boat and walked on the water he was fine as long as Jesus was in his line of vision. Once he looked at the waves, he lost the plot (Matthew 14:28–30).

God's people following Moses in the desert sometimes focused more on circumstances—lack of water, boring food—than God's provision. They paid heavily for their rebellion (Numbers 11:1–35).

Whether the waves are rocking our boat or we're experiencing a perceived lack of something vital, let's focus on Jesus. We'll find that he will enable us to walk on the water, meet our needs or help us to triumph in the face of that need.

CP

God's got the steering wheel

For if Joshua had given them rest, God would not have spoken later about another day. There remains, then, a Sabbath-rest for the people of God; for anyone who enters God's rest also rests from his own work, just as God did from his.

The progress of God's people through Genesis and Exodus seems highly convoluted. Abraham left his homeland and travelled to Canaan, the land God had promised. His family grew but never owned the land. Then, Abraham's grandson, Jacob, and his family suffered a severe famine. Were they all going to be wiped out? One of Jacob's sons, Joseph, was rejected by his brothers, enslaved, imprisoned and became Prime Minister of Egypt! Egypt had food, so Jacob and his family went there to live.

In Egypt, God's people flourished, but this was not the land that God had promised. Eventually it all turned sour and God called Moses to lead the people back to Canaan. Forty years of wandering later, Moses' work was finished and the people arrived at the border. Joshua was God's choice of leader to take them into the land and help them take possession of it.

It must have been confusing for the people at times. Where was God? Where was his promise of rest? We have the huge advantage today of being able to look back and see the whole story. It is clear that God was guiding events and working out his purposes.

Is your life confusing at the moment? Maybe there are things that God has promised but you can't see any prospect of their fulfilment. Are you wondering where God is? Let these lessons from history reassure you. God has not abandoned you. You will eventually see him bringing everything together and you'll be able to echo Joshua's words: '…You know with all your heart and soul that not one of all the good promises the Lord your God gave you has failed. Every promise has been fulfilled; not one has failed' (Joshua 23:14).

Thank you, God, that your hand is on the steering wheel of history.

CP

Perfect sacrifice

Therefore, since we have a great high priest who has gone through the heavens, Jesus the Son of God, let us hold firmly to the faith we profess. For we do not have a high priest who is unable to sympathise with our weaknesses.

Wanted: one great high priest. Qualities needed:

- total perfection
- able to withstand the most acute temptation
- able to identify with sinful men and women
- ready to endure poverty, scorn, torture, grisly death.

Priests and sacrifices were big issues in the lives of God's people. Priests were the intermediaries between God and ordinary men and women. When a person sins, it affects their relationship with God. To remove that barrier the person concerned would bring an animal to the priest for him to offer as a sacrifice. Hebrews 9:22 explains it like this: 'In fact, the law requires that nearly everything be cleansed with blood, and without the shedding of blood there is no forgiveness.'

All this blood-and-guts activity in the Old Testament was a mere copy of what Jesus would do on our behalf. He is the great high priest who not only was the intermediary but also became the sacrifice. Only someone who is fully God, therefore without sin, and fully man is adequate for this job.

How incredibly fortunate we are to live this side of the cross, but we can fall into the trap of taking forgiveness for granted and forgetting what it cost. I think I would take my own sin more seriously if a living creature had to die in front of my eyes in order for me to be forgiven. The next time you're saying sorry to God, take a few minutes to imagine buying a lamb and watching it being slaughtered for you. Try to enter into the seriousness of sin.

Thank you, Lord, for dying a horrible death in my place so that I can receive complete forgiveness.

CP

Waiting for baby

When God made his promise to Abraham, since there was no one greater for him to swear by, he swore by himself, saying, 'I will surely bless you and give you many descendants.' And so after waiting patiently, Abraham received what was promised.

Isn't waiting one of the most excruciating things we have to cope with? Whether it's children eagerly anticipating Christmas or a sick person waiting for pain to lift and health to return—waiting doesn't come easily to the human spirit.

Abraham had to wait 25 years to receive the fulfilment of the promise of a son with Sarah (Genesis 15:1–6; 21:1–2). As the years relentlessly ticked by, Abraham and Sarah must have gone through agonies of confusion and disappointment, wondering when God was going to act. Finally, in Genesis 16, they decided that God needed their help. They took matters into their own hands with disastrous results, but God would not be rushed. His promise came to fruition at the right time, just as he said it would.

Waiting doesn't fit in with our culture—life is getting faster and faster. Waiting appears to be a waste of time. If things aren't working out well, we need to fix it immediately. These stories of our spiritual ancestors are valuable for us today as they put our waiting times into perspective.

Are you perplexed about God and his promises? Does it feel like your prayers hit the ceiling? Be encouraged by Abraham and Sarah's story. They didn't always get it right, but God kept his side of the bargain. Baby Isaac was born and, because of the long wait, it was obvious to everyone that this was God's special gift to the proud parents. That meant God got the credit for it, not Abraham and Sarah.

God is at work even when we can't see it and the waiting feels long. Hang in there. As Paul reminds us, 'We live by faith, not by sight' (2 Corinthians 5:7).

Lord, help me live according to your timetable and not my own.

CP

The clock is ticking

There have been many of those priests, since death prevented them from continuing in office; but because Jesus lives for ever, he has a permanent priesthood. Therefore he is able to save… because he always lives to intercede for them.

I adore musicals and went to see a performance of *The Reason Why*, which is the life story of Robert Laidlaw, an influential Christian businessman and philanthropist in New Zealand. This week I was shocked to hear of the sudden death of the writer of that musical. He was only 54. During his life, he used theatre and music in a highly effective ministry with young people, as well as reaching a much broader audience.

There are two significant facts that affect every single person on this earth. We are all born and we all die. We have a limited time to fulfil the role that God has uniquely created us for, whether it's writing musicals, creating a loving and positive home environment or pursuing a career.

One day, just like the Old Testament priests, death will prevent us from continuing in office. This needn't send us into panic mode, but rather should give us a heightened respect for each day of our lives. Every hour is a gift to be relished and invested for God's kingdom.

Ecclesiastes 9:10 is a constant challenge to me: 'Whatever your hand finds to do, do it with all your might…'. In all honesty we have to admit that some of our activities are not at all inspiring—boring might be a better word—but bringing God into them can infuse them with new meaning. This verse is also a stimulus to examine how we spend our time. Just think, if you died today, would you have regrets about the way you invested your life? If so, don't waste time wallowing in guilt for the past, resolve to make the most of the future.

Take a moment to bring today to Jesus and ask for his help and guidance to use it for his kingdom and pleasure.

CP

Number one bridge builder

But the ministry Jesus has received is as superior to theirs [the Old Testament priests] as the covenant of which he is mediator is superior to the old one, and it is founded on better promises.

New Zealand is a yachting paradise—picturesque waterways and inlets abound. All this water creates mighty challenges for the transport system. A bridge was built across one of the main harbours to enable thousands of commuters to get into Auckland city to work. Bridges form vital links. A bridge out of action causes chaos and frustration—access is denied.

The Latin word for priest is *pontifex*, which means bridge builder. The Old Testament priests were the link between God and ordinary men and women. The bridges they built were unsatisfactory because the builders were sinners themselves. Access to God was limited. Only the high priest could enter the most holy place to meet with God once a year.

Jesus built the ultimate bridge for us. With him as our mediator, we walk confidently into the holy of holies and enjoy all the benefits of the new covenant. The old covenant in Moses' time was based on obedience to external laws. People proved unable to keep their side of the bargain (v. 9b). The glorious new covenant is written in the hearts of believers (v. 10), thus giving an inner compulsion to obey and please God.

Why is it that many people's concept of Christianity is stuck in the Old Testament? They think of rules—lots of dos and don'ts. However, the new covenant is based on a relationship, not rule-keeping (v. 10b).

What are we communicating about our faith to others? Do they see someone living joyfully by grace or bowed down by rules? Sometimes Christians are characterized by what we don't do rather than positive action. We ought to be the most liberated and happy people on earth! Think of all that Jesus has done for us!

Lord, help me show a true picture of your new covenant of grace in the way I live today.

CP

Unleash the power!

Without the shedding of blood there is no forgiveness... But now he has appeared once for all at the end of the ages to do away with sin by the sacrifice of himself.

Forgiveness is powerful. It can break the cycle of vengeance. Unfortunately, the converse is also true. Lack of forgiveness casts its sinister shadow deep and wide. World conflicts are fuelled by lack of forgiveness—each side insisting on their right to retaliate. 'We must defend ourselves' is the clarion call, even if that means offensive action towards the enemy. Neither party is willing to back down. The Rwandan genocide, the meltdown of former Yugoslavia, the conflict in Northern Ireland are vivid examples of hatred fostered throughout generations.

How amazingly refreshing it was to see Nelson Mandela emerge from 27 years' imprisonment with a huge smile on his face. He was not breathing fire or inciting his allies to avenge the wrongs committed against him. Rather, he willingly worked with his old enemies. Political analysts were predicting a bloodbath but, instead, great gains were made in healing decades of injustice.

These principles hold true in personal and family conflicts also. Two of my aunts had a disagreement and didn't speak to each other for ten years. The next time they met, one of them was dead and the other attended the funeral—much too little, much too late.

If only forgiveness were easier! This chapter shows how God orchestrated an elaborate system of sacrifice at the time of Moses for men and women to acknowledge the seriousness of their sin and receive forgiveness (vv. 1–10). This prefigured Christ and his perfect offering. Our forgiveness came at an unbelievably high cost.

Let's not be guilty of belittling that cost and taking our forgiveness lightly. Let's be truly thankful that our sin has been dealt with. As we've received mercy, we need to extend that to others. Don't be like my aunts and allow resentment to poison your mind and heart. That poison will fester and infect other relationships. You'll deeply regret it.

Read Matthew 6:14–15.

CP

Standing or sitting?

Day after day every priest stands and performs his religious duties… But when this priest [Jesus] had offered for all time one sacrifice for sins, he sat down at the right hand of God.

The Old Testament priests stood because their work was never finished. They had to keep offering sacrifices day after day. Jesus, in contrast, finished his work and sat down in the place of majesty. No further sacrifice was necessary.

This is a profound truth, but many of us pay lip-service to it. We confess our sins, but still feel nagging guilt. Do you ever subconsciously want to do something as penance and somehow make up for your misdemeanours—to make a renewed effort to pray or read your Bible or be especially nice to people? Those are great things to aspire to, but we need to have the right motive—worship and service, not as a substitute for Jesus' sacrifice.

Satan takes malicious delight in reminding us of our failures. He is quick to throw his 'flaming arrows' into our minds at unguarded moments—those poisonous phrases that kill our joy and rob us of peace (Ephesians 6:16)—'You're a failure. You'll never be a good Christian. Look at what you've done.' All too often we listen to him instead of God who has promised to remember our sins no more (Hebrews 10:17).

God has given us ways to protect our minds, just as he has given us skin to protect our bodies. I was recently helping to build a house in very dirty, muddy conditions in Fiji. I got some cuts on my leg, so I quickly cleaned them and put plasters on. A friend also got cut but didn't take the same precautions. Mine healed up fast. His festered and required more radical treatment.

When Satan accuses us, we need to quickly 'clean the wound'—turn our minds to God's truth. His promises form a barrier against Satan's arrows. They are deflected away so that they cannot penetrate and do damage (Matthew 4:1–11).

Read Psalm 103:8–13.

CP

Love God, love people

Let us draw near to God... let us consider how we may spur one another on towards love and good deeds... let us encourage one another—and all the more as you see the Day approaching.

Here are two great truths in tandem: our relationship with God and our relationships with people. As we walk with God day by day, he will urge us to be involved with people. Our involvement with people will reveal needs and drive us to God again to receive his strength and wisdom.

When Jesus called his first disciples, the aim was for them to be with him and be sent out to preach (Mark 3:14). The relationship with him was the priority, then their ministry to others.

The immensity of the needs of those around us can very easily overwhelm those with compassionate hearts. They give themselves tirelessly to help relieve suffering, but sometimes suffer burn-out themselves. For these ones, it's hard to take time out to come away and be refreshed by God. However, even Jesus himself withdrew from multitudes of needy people in order to spend time with his Father (Luke 5:15–16).

Others of us find it easier to spend time with God, but we draw back from costly involvement with people. Some friends of mine were involved in youth ministry. When the teenagers came to the house for a meeting, the wife was downstairs, making coffee and chatting, whereas the husband was upstairs praying—only appearing when it was time to give the message. He realized that he was acting out of fear of being out of his comfort zone. Prayer is vitally important, but not to be used as a means of keeping distance in relationships with people. He decided to make sure that his prayer time finished before the young people arrived and, as he stepped out and made himself vulnerable, God gave him a much more fruitful ministry.

Lord, help me go deeper with you and the people you've given me to care for.

CP

Faith muscles in action

By faith Abraham, when called to go to a place he would later receive as his inheritance, obeyed and went, even though he did not know where he was going… For he was looking forward to the city with foundations, whose architect and builder is God.

Today, the world is a global village. We jet about visiting exotic places with comparative ease whereas previous generations barely left their birthplace. Because of this mindset, we can miss the enormity of Abraham's adventure. It's true that peoples have always migrated to find better land and opportunities, but this doesn't take away from Abraham's gigantic risk he took because of his faith.

Just because God told him to, he ventured out to the great unknown. The only guarantee he had was God's promise. Abraham experienced many ups and downs and challenges to his faith (Genesis 12—25). So, what kept him going? What stopped him retreating back to the safety of home? His focus was on looking forward to what God had promised. If he had looked back, he would never have made it. Remember Lot's wife (Genesis 19:23–26).

God calls us to a great adventure with him. He doesn't guarantee a smooth ride, but he does promise a destination that is out of this world.

Are you ready for an exciting adventure or are you overly cautious and want to know how it's going to turn out before you put your toe in the water?

Hebrews 11 gives a stirring litany of God's Academy Award winners—ordinary men and women who believed God. They kept their focus on him and not on their circumstances or disappointments. God probably won't ask us to be willing to be sawn in two or flogged today, but he certainly presents us with opportunities to exercise our faith muscles. Muscles need regular use to be effective otherwise they become flabby. Even the smallest step of faith will help tone those muscles.

Lord, help me keep my eyes on you today and take those faith steps that you have prepared for me.

CP

Eternity in a throwaway world

Therefore, since we are receiving a kingdom that cannot be shaken, let us be thankful, and so worship God acceptably with reverence and awe, for our 'God is a consuming fire.'

I don't relish the picture of God as a consuming fire. I much prefer the Good Shepherd image, but that is only a partial vision. The 'therefore' in this verse refers to a grim warning. Those who turn away from God will be judged. All they trust in will turn to dust. Only what is eternal will remain (10:25–27).

What, in our throwaway world, does last for ever? Just three things: God, his word and people. The things that the world craves—fame, money, beauty, expensive houses and cars—will be revealed as tawdry trinkets. Those who've invested in true riches will have the immense satisfaction of knowing that their lives have not been wasted. What we treasure now will be exposed to fire later—will it burn or be revealed as gold?

Our relationship with God is priority number one. The first commandment is to have no other gods before him or, as Jesus expressed it, 'Love the Lord your God with all your heart and with all your soul and with all your mind and with all your strength' (Mark 12:30). If we love God, then we will want to know what he says in his word. Love of God and his word gives us glimpses of his passionate heart for people. Inevitably, we will be led to serve his people and introduce others to him.

We are urged to worship God acceptably. Romans 12:1 gives us a clue what this might mean—giving ourselves fully to him as a living sacrifice. When we sing words such as 'Take me, mould me, fill me', we have to mean them, so our outward worship reflects our inner desire. God was scathing towards those who honoured him with their lips, when their hearts were far from him (Isaiah 29:13).

Do you need to re-examine your priorities in the light of these truths? Do it now, don't delay.

CP

Grand finale

May the God of peace, who through the blood of the eternal covenant brought back from the dead our Lord Jesus, that great Shepherd of the sheep, equip you with everything good for doing his will.

These truths are music to the ears of discouraged and stressed souls. Our God is the God of peace. Through Jesus he has not only given us peace with himself, but he can also give us peace in the most difficult and anxiety-ridden situations (Philippians 4:6–7).

He is also the God of life. Jesus conquered death for us and we enjoy eternal life through him (1 Corinthians 15:54–56). He is the guide and enabler. When he calls us to exciting and fulfilling roles, he promises to give us the gifts that we need to do his will.

Jesus is the great Shepherd of the sheep—tenderness, protection, guidance, provision and love are encompassed in this phrase. There is a vulnerability about sheep that makes this image even more poignant. Supermen and superwomen are not needed. God's grace shows up best in weak people. God's word to Paul was: 'My grace is sufficient for you, for my power is made perfect in weakness' (2 Corinthians 12:7–10).

Throughout these two weeks looking at Hebrews, we've observed God's plan of action. Abraham ventured forth to an unknown destination. Moses led the Exodus from Egypt and inaugurated the sacrificial system of worship. It's as though these pictures from the Old Testament are in black and white, then comes *la pièce de résistance*—Jesus, who transforms everything into glorious Technicolor. His law is now written in our hearts, not on stone tablets. We have free access to his throne, not via a priest.

God is still working out his purposes. His plan culminates with Jesus' return—not as a baby, but in a blaze of majestic glory (2 Thessalonians 1:7–10).

Let's make sure that we and all we love are ready for that return. In the meantime, what do you need today? Peace, life, guidance, enabling? Ask the great Shepherd of the sheep.

CP

Come on, everybody!

Praise O servants of the Lord; praise the name of the Lord. Blessed be the name of the Lord... Who is like the Lord our God... Praise the Lord!

Have you ever come to church feeling rather down and found that you are lifted and carried by other people's praise until you begin to flow with praise yourself? The service says, in effect, 'We're going to celebrate and praise God now, so come on everybody and join in!' That is very much what the psalmist is doing here.

I have struggled for years with the book of Psalms. Early on, I expected them to be mostly praise, but I soon found that many of them consist largely of complaint or lament, though many of these do finish up by expressing faith in God and his goodness. Then I expected the cheerful psalms to be expressions of praise to God, but realized that many of them are exhortations to praise God, rather than addressing praise directly to God. Thus, in order for me to use them to express praise to God, face to face, I have to alter them a little in my mind, changing, for example, 'God is great' to 'God, you are great'.

I have found two ways round (or through) these struggles. The first has been to realize that praising someone to their face is not the only valid form of praise: it is also true praise when I praise them to someone else. It is one form of praise to say, 'Mary, you are a wonderful cook', but it is also genuine praise to say, 'Mary is a wonderful cook'. Thus, the psalms that say 'God is great' are also real praise.

The second helpful insight has been the discovery that hearing somebody else extolling a person's good qualities can increase your own admiration and appreciation of that person. In the same way, reading or saying the psalms can draw out our admiration, gratitude and praise for God.

Why not read Psalms in the coming two weeks and praise the Lord?

MD

Why praise?

Praise the Lord! How good it is to sing praises to our God; for he is gracious, and a song of praise is fitting.

This psalm tells us that it is good to praise God for who he is and urges us to do so, too. I don't suppose that I am the only person to have wondered why it is so good to keep praising God. It seems from other parts of the Bible that God wants us to worship and praise him. There is not the same problem with thanksgiving—it is obviously good to thank God for what he gives and does for us. There is no problem either with the idea of saying, 'I love you' to God when we do love him. To think of God wanting us to praise him, though, can seem a little odd.

Children look for praise partly because they are insecure about their strengths and weaknesses and need encouragement. Adults benefit from encouragement, too, but we hope that they have become sufficiently secure not to keep looking for praise or fishing for compliments. When the Bible exhorts us to praise God, is this God fishing for compliments? Surely God does not need us to boost his confidence! The very idea is ludicrous.

Why, then, are we exhorted to praise him? I think the answer is that praising God is for our benefit more than his. The appropriate response to greatness and goodness is awe, wonder and delight, and he is infinitely good and great. If we offer our admiration and praise, they will not be wasted on something or someone unworthy and, if we do not see the worth and admire it, we will have missed something.

So we come back to where we started, in Psalm 147. It is good to praise God, for he is gracious—and great and loving and a whole lot more besides. So, even if we feel self-conscious about it sometimes, let's keep practising, for God's glory and our own benefit, too.

Sing or say the words of a favourite hymn of praise to God.

MD

Who on earth made all this?

Rejoice in the Lord... Let all the earth fear the Lord; let all the inhabitants of the world stand in awe of him. For he spoke, and it came to be; he commanded, and it stood firm.

Some of the inventions that have been of the greatest benefit to human life seem quite simple once you know about them. The wheel is one good example. Paper and fire are others. In each case, the idea is simple, but what put it into someone's head? I don't really know, but I think it very likely that the idea was triggered by something the person saw. Something presumably happened naturally or accidentally and they then realized how it could be repeated and used.

However, when God created the world, there was nothing outside him to give him ideas. It all came from him. The more we discover about the world, the more amazing it seems, but God didn't merely discover it, he thought the whole thing up in the first place! This 'creation out of nothing' fills me with awe and wonder at the greatness of our creator.

Another thing that strikes me forcibly is that God not only conceived the idea of creation, but also brought it into existence. A relative of my husband used to invent useful objects for the home. We have some ingenious tablemats made by him. Unfortunately, he did not make a lot of money from his inventions because, even when he himself managed to make the prototypes and obtain the patents, he could not persuade anyone to invest enough money in them to market his creations. What a contrast with our creator! God did not need the help of a backer or a manufacturer, but did it all himself. He said, 'Let there be light, earth, sea, life...' and there was light, earth, sea, life and all the rest. How can we do anything other than worship, bowing or kneeling before the Lord, our maker?

Creator God, we bow before you and acknowledge your greatness.

MD

Such love!

O give thanks to the Lord, for he is good, for his steadfast love endures for ever. O give thanks to the God of gods, for his steadfast love endures for ever.

Psalm 136 declares God's love over and over again. Throughout the psalm, the psalmist remembers lots of things that God has done in the Israelites' history that reveal the greatness and constancy of his love. After each one, in every verse, he uses the same words: 'for his steadfast love endures for ever'.

I was slightly irritated by all this repetition at first, until I remembered how it feels to fall in love. In particular, I thought of how it feels when you realize that you are dearly loved by someone who is very special to you. It can feel like walking on air, with the words 'He loves me; he really, really loves me' (or something of that kind) going round and round in your head.

I then thought of how I valued the security of my parents' love and other relationships in which I have felt quite overwhelmed by people's love and care for me. When I remembered those feelings, the idea of declaring such love over and over again didn't seem either irritating or self-conscious.

Human love is never absolutely perfect, but God's love always is. When we first discover God's love, our heads and hearts may ring with, 'He loves me; he really, really loves me', but not only then. As we go on in our journey with God, we will keep on discovering new aspects of his love. We shall probably at times experience the sense of wonder that this intense, active love still continues unabated, even when we let him down—again! We may thrill over and over again to the words 'his love endures for ever'. The greatness and constancy of God's love and the fact that it is there for ever are worthy of endless repetition.

Thank you, Father, that your steadfast love does endure for ever.

MD

Praise when life is tough?

I will bless the Lord at all times; his praise shall continually be in my mouth.

At any time, on any day, some people in the world will be finding life pleasant, peaceful and joyful, while others are suffering pain, anxiety or fear. When life is enjoyable for us, we may find it relatively easy to praise God, but what about when it is tough? Here the psalmist sets us the example of praising God at all times. All times will include those days or periods in our lives when things are really hard—times of disappointment, illness, loss or drudgery. Can we honestly praise God under such circumstances?

We don't usually doubt the rightness of praising God when life is pleasant for us, but at those very times there will be others somewhere for whom it is tough. Is it still right for us to praise God then, even though others are having a hard time? Yes, it must be, because the reason for our praise is that God is actually good and loving and worthy of praise.

So what about when we are the ones who are suffering? What is different then? Our circumstances and feelings have changed, but the character of God has not changed. If he was worthy of praise before, he is still worthy of praise now, even if we cannot understand what he is doing (or not doing!)

When life feels tough we can be honest, not pretending to have feelings of enjoyment or happiness that we do not have. Yet it is still possible, though not always easy, to continue to affirm and trust in the goodness of God, who will one day bring us out of our present difficulty and draw good out of it for us (see Romans 8:28).

Gracious Father, when we find life tough, we are sometimes tempted to doubt your love or your power. Please help us not only to hang on to you at those times, but also to praise you in all circumstances, through Jesus Christ, our Lord. Amen

MD

Praise the God of rescue!

Make a joyful noise to God, all the earth... Come and see what God has done; he is awesome in his deeds among mortals... Come and hear, all you who fear God, and I will tell what he has done for me.

In the film *Titanic*, the hero and heroine find, in their love for each other, an enormous growth in maturity and freedom. After the ship hits the iceberg, the hero ensures that his beloved is safe, but dies himself, drowning in the icy water. Later the heroine says of him, 'He saved me in every way possible.' Although this is bound to be an exaggeration when said about any human being, it is no exaggeration about God. We can see parallels with *Titanic*'s hero in Jesus, who, at the cost of his life, has made possible for us all wholeness, peace, safety and freedom, which we experience partially in this life and fully in the next.

The psalmist does not, of course, know about Jesus, but in this psalm he encourages people to praise God for what he does know of God's many acts of salvation and rescue. He reminds them of how God rescued his people from Egypt and parted the Red Sea for them to cross to safety and freedom. He reminds them, too, that although there have been many tough and dangerous times since then, God has 'brought [them] out into a spacious place'. His own response is to thank and bless God for what he has done.

We also do well to keep reminding ourselves of what God has done for us—both in Jesus' life, death and resurrection and in our own personal history. This can be helpful, not only because praise is intrinsically good, but also because it strengthens our faith.

Father, we are so glad that you are a rescuing God. We thank and praise you for all you have done to rescue us. Help me to tell others what you have done for me.

MD

Thank God!

O give thanks to the Lord, for he is good; for his steadfast love endures for ever. Let the redeemed of the Lord say so, those he redeemed from trouble.

Thanks expresses appreciation of a gift, whereas praise expresses appreciation of the giver. Yet, it is also true that thanks and praise readily flow into each other as the quality and appropriateness of the gift can reveal something of the nature of the giver.

It is good to thank God often for several reasons.

- *It is always right and appropriate to express gratitude for what we are given.* We feel guilty when we do not write our thank you letters and when someone does not thank us for a gift, we wonder if something is wrong.
- *It builds our trust in God, because it reminds us of his faithfulness and kindness to us.* When we count our blessings, it does sometimes surprise us what the Lord has done. Paul says of Abraham '... he grew strong in his faith as he gave glory to God' (Romans 4:20).
- *It helps to develop the relationship with him.* Any conversation helps to build a relationship, but thanksgiving to God expresses the basis of his relationship to us—as our creator and giver to us, his dependants.
- *It reminds us that he is with us, noticing what we need and providing for us.* This strengthens our awareness that he knows and cares about us.
- *It helps us to be more contented and joyful people.* Then, we appreciate what we have received, rather than complain about what we haven't got.

Considering the quality of God's gifts and the greatness of the giver, it is perhaps surprising that we so easily forget to thank him. Establishing one, or both, of the following habits might help.

Thank God for at least five things each day. Once a day (in the evening?) ask, 'What am I most grateful for today?' then thank God for it.

MD

Come on, self!

Bless the Lord, O my soul. O Lord my God, you are very great… I will sing to the Lord as long as I live; I will sing praise to my God while I have being. May my meditation be pleasing to him, for I rejoice in the Lord… Bless the Lord, O my soul. Praise the Lord.

It is interesting when watching a tennis match to see that many players say something like 'Come on!' to themselves, often clenching a fist and making a firm movement with the arm. They talk to themselves to urge themselves on to do their best, either when they have made a mistake or when they are near to winning a significant game or set and want to stop themselves slackening off too soon.

That is what the psalmist is doing in this psalm, urging himself to make the appropriate response to God's nature. He then reminds himself of where he sees God's greatness and goodness in the way he has made and sustains the world and all its life and tells himself to praise the Lord.

Anglicans will recognize the words 'it is our duty and our joy, at all times and in all places to give you thanks and praise'. When thanks and praise are pure joy, they bubble out of us effortlessly. Much of the time, however, there is some degree of duty and effort about it. Even when we are praying, we are so busy asking for things, saying sorry and telling God what we are thinking and feeling that praise easily is squeezed out. At those times, we need to urge ourselves on to praise God and thank him for his many good gifts.

What are the one or two things that you value most about God today? (Be as honest as possible about what you really do value, not what you think you ought to value!) Pause for a moment to ponder these things now, then respond in whatever form of thanks or praise seems good to you.

MD

Merciful and forgiving Lord

The Lord is merciful and gracious, slow to anger and abounding in steadfast love... He does not deal with us according to our sins, nor repay us according to our iniquities... as far as the east is from the west, so far he removes our transgressions from us.

One of the recent bright lights in the dark troubles in Northern Ireland was Gordon Wilson, a Christian who forgave those who had planted the bomb that killed his daughter. Many people admired him for this. I don't know how long it took Gordon Wilson to forgive fully, but human forgiving is almost always a process. Even if we manage to do most of it in one go, we often find later some aspects we missed out, some loose ends that still need to be tidied up. However, when we have fully forgiven someone, we will:

- not tell anyone else what they did to us
- not try to make them feel guilty
- never bring up the subject again

God's nature is forgiving, so he is able to forgive immediately and always forgives fully (v. 12).

Although Gordon Wilson could show forgiveness towards those who killed his daughter, he was not in a position to show them mercy. He did not have any power over the bombers and my dictionary defines mercy as 'forbearance towards someone who is in one's power'. Between us and God, however, it is the case that we are not only constantly offending and grieving him, but also always in his power. What a blessing it is to us, therefore, that God is merciful. The fact that God's very nature is merciful means that mercy is not something he sometimes shows and sometimes doesn't. We can't catch him unawares being unmerciful! He is always merciful, always forbearing. We have only to compare that to our own attitudes to realize how wonderful he is.

Father, we marvel and delight in your merciful nature. Thank you for setting us free from sin and its consequences.

MD

Praise the Lord for his compassion

As a father has compassion for his children, so the Lord has compassion for those who fear him. For he knows how we were made; he remembers that we are dust... But the steadfast love of the Lord is from everlasting to everlasting on those who fear him.

Compassion involves feeling sorrow or pain concerning the sufferings of someone else. The better you know someone and their circumstances, the better you can understand how their suffering is affecting them. The more you love them, the more you are likely to suffer because of their suffering. Surely the God of infinite compassion, who knows and understands each of us perfectly and who loves us as his children, suffers alongside us in our pain?

Compassion and kindness go hand in hand because kindness tries to minimize someone's pain. Another characteristic of kindness is that it does more than might reasonably be expected.

I remember an occasion when I confided to someone one of my fears about which I felt very feeble and ashamed. She did not make me feel foolish, but showed me that she understood fear and offered gentle, practical advice on how to handle it. She also pointed me to this psalm. I had not expected her to be harsh, but she showed me such compassion and kindness that it took me by surprise as she took my fear seriously and sought to help me. When I reflected on this afterwards, I was moved to tears—not only because of her own compassion and kindness, but because it enabled me to believe and trust that God would treat me at least as kindly as she had. When other people show us acts of kindness, we catch glimpses of the kindness of God.

For the love of God is broader
Than the measures of man's mind;
And the heart of the Eternal
Is most wonderfully kind.

F.W. FABER (1814–63)

MD

Praise using the body

Let the children of Zion rejoice in their King. Let them praise his name with dancing, making melody to him with tambourine and lyre. For the Lord takes pleasure in his people.

How often do you worship with dancing, tambourines and lyres in your church? The psalms were originally written for use when God's people worshipped together. Dancing was clearly sometimes part of their worship, as were clapping hands (Psalm 47:1) and bowing or kneeling, too (Psalm 95:6). It seems to have been normal to use the body for corporate praise and worship.

We use our bodies in prayer, too—we stand, sit or kneel for different parts of our church services. In some churches, people may bow, or genuflect, or make the sign of the cross; in others, they may dance, clap, or raise their hands. Most of these actions started in order to express something to God—sometimes awe and respect, sometimes delight and celebration, but always a response to who God is and what he has done.

The principle of using our bodies to praise God is a good and biblical one, as this psalm indicates. We might do well to use some of them in our personal prayer times, too. I have danced to worship tapes in the past (not nowadays, as I am more creaky!) and I sometimes vary my posture. Why not try standing up and looking upwards as you pray or hold out your hands as a symbol of reaching out to God or even dancing?

A ballerina once said, when asked what her dancing meant, 'If I could put it into words, I would not need to dance it.' We, too, might find that we can express praise with our bodies more deeply than with our words. It is well worth a try, asking God to show us what would enrich our praise now.

Father, help me not to condemn actions that help others to praise you and to be open to any new ways of praising you into which you are leading me.

MD

Praise through music

Praise him with trumpet sound... with lute and harp!... with tambourine and dance... with strings and pipe!... with clanging cymbals... with loud clashing cymbals! Let everything that breathes praise the Lord!

In fact, the psalmist might as well say, 'Praise him with the whole orchestra!' He is exhorting musicians to use their instruments to praise God.

Music does things for us and in us at least partly by engaging the emotions. Whether on instruments or with our voices, we can express our emotions in music, by our choice of piece and by the way we play it or by the way we extemporize. In our musicmaking, we may express exhilaration, sadness, uncertainty, anger... and praise. When we know what feelings we want to communicate to God, we can express them in music. Whether we are playing or listening, the emotion of a piece of music and the way in which it is being played can catch us up in itself to produce or enhance this emotion in us.

When we find it hard to praise God—maybe because we are tired or preoccupied or simply feeling a bit flat—music can lift us into thoughts and feelings we would not otherwise have. This happens especially when we are listening to music rather than playing it because others, the composer and instrumentalists, are making some of the effort for us and leading us into their praise. Playing a short piece of music that will quieten us or turn our hearts towards God can be a helpful start to a prayer time.

It is helpful to build up a stock of resources that you know have particular effects on you and keep three or four tapes or CDs of these pieces in the car or in the place where you normally pray.

Thank you, Lord, for the gift of music and the ways in which your Holy Spirit has inspired many composers and players to produce music that helps us to praise you.

MD

Silent praise and delight

The heavens are telling the glory of God; and the firmament proclaims his handiwork... There is no speech, nor are there words; their voice is not heard; yet their voice goes out through all the earth, and their words to the end of the world.

Creation praises God simply by being there—beautiful and with each part fulfilling its function as it was made to do. As we contemplate the world, we come to appreciate the greatness of our creator. Thus, the heavens (sun, moon and stars) tell the glory of God, not in audible words, but by silently pointing us to God's greatness.

In the same way, we can bring praise and glory to God silently, simply by being what God made us to be, becoming more like him and living our lives in the ways he wants. There is another way of praising God silently, which I find most helpful myself. I call it 'silent delighting' in God. It involves pondering God—his nature or some aspect of his character, such as his goodness or mercy—and admiring, enjoying, delighting in who he is and what he is like. Almost anything can lead us into this contemplation and silent delighting—a beautiful view, an event, experience or, importantly, scripture. We need not put words to our thoughts and feelings, merely pour ourselves into our delight and appreciation of God, perhaps with a sigh, a 'Wow!' or an 'Ah'. The nearest comparison I can think of to this is the love, pride and delight that we feel in our hearts when we take time to contemplate our children or someone else we love involved in some activity or when they are asleep. I had hoped to find a psalm that expressed this silent delighting more clearly, but I have not found one, so just try it and see for yourself.

Take time today to delight in God—perhaps on a walk in a park, or focusing on a Psalm. Allow God to touch your heart as you spend time appreciating him.

MD

Aspects of angels

Hagar stopped to rest at a spring in the desert… While she was there, the angel of the Lord came to her.

Christmas angels are everywhere again, aren't they? They glisten from the tops of Christmas trees and float on card-holding wires. Paper ones come home sticky and glittery from school at the end of term. They are pretty and non-threatening and they always have wings.

Another thing about Christmas angels is that they are usually female, about three feet high, wearing cut down white sheets with tinsel stapled round the hem. The Angel of the North, arms outstretched, keeping watch over the North East of England, is an awesome sight and perhaps more relevant than those tinselly Christmas ones.

Deep in the consciousness of not only Christians but also those who deny the existence of God, there is a feeling that angels really do exist. In some way that we don't understand, they watch over us, protect us, interact with us.

Not counting the 'winged creatures' at Eden's gates, the first angel recorded in the Bible comes with no pomp or ceremony whatsoever to bring a message of hope directly from God to a disgraced slave girl. So, what can we glean from this first recorded angelic visitation? For starters, any suggestion of angels looking different from humans is immediately dispelled. This girl is the first person to see an angel. Surely a little gasp would have been allowable, but no—a perfectly friendly conversation takes place between the angel and Hagar at the side of the dusty road.

During these early crucial days when the dynasty of Abraham is being established. there is a very real sense of angels being round every corner. A 'Quick! Stop her, she's getting away' call comes through on the direct line and, whoosh, he's there to turn this unhappy girl back to Sarai and Abraham's home, so that God's intricate plan for humanity is not destroyed by human frailty before it really gets going!

Dear Father, help me to be open to words from you from unexpected people in unexpected places.

BP

Action men angels

The two angels said to Lot, 'The Lord has heard many terrible things about the people of Sodom, and he has sent us here to destroy the city. Take your family and leave... So the angels took Lot, his wife, and his two daughters by the hand and led them out of the city.

There are angels popping up everywhere throughout the early books of the Bible. They are usually decidedly male and frequently heavily involved in the action. Take, for example, the two who are given parts in the opening scenes of the founding of the tribe of Israel (Genesis 18). When they first appear, they seem to be acting as bodyguards to an exceptional, early popping down to earth by the Lord. Headquarters, in its infinite wisdom, has obviously felt that nothing short of a visit from the boss will do to convince Abraham's octogenarian wife Sarai that she is going to have a child.

These angels, having eaten heartily (yes, it would seem that they have healthy appetites when in human form), leave the Lord and Abraham and set off on foot (still not a wing in sight) towards Sodom, a city God has condemned because of its sinfulness. Their mission? To help Lot and his family escape from the city and get away before God sends burning sulphur down on the town. Increasingly they seem to be the original 'A team' as they race through the streets, hauling Lot, his wife and two daughters by the hand, urging them to run ever faster. Out of the town the two angels urgently give instructions to 'Run for your lives' and promise to hold off razing Sodom to the ground until the family have safely reached the nearby village of Zoar.

We've just got to do something about these non-threatening, tinselly ideas of ours, haven't we?

Father, open my eyes to the possibilities of angels being around just when and where I don't expect to see them and the idea that they could be a lot more directly involved with what happens to my life than I think.

BP

Angels with attitude

The Lord said: 'I am sending an angel to protect you and to lead you into the land I have ready for you. Carefully obey everything the angel says, because I am giving him complete authority, and he won't tolerate rebellion.'

The angel was holding a walking stick, and he touched the meat and the bread with the end of the stick. Flames jumped from the rock and burnt up the meat and the bread.

Before reading this command in Exodus from God to Moses' children of Israel, I had always assumed that angels never departed from the script that they had been given in heaven. Here, it would seem, is an angel with attitude! Does this mean that they have other human attributes when they are among us here on earth? Do they ever twinkle, for example? Share a joke? Get fed up? The one mentioned here sounds as though he is capable of getting angry.

Then, what do you make of the opening words to Gideon (Judges 6:12) by his angelic visitor when, watching him threshing wheat in a pit to keep it hidden from the enemy, he greets him as a 'strong warrior'! Surely there has to be a touch of ironic humour there.

We know that Jesus wept and laughed and got angry and frustrated, so maybe the angels do, too, and perhaps they enjoyed some of the tricks God let them perform. There is a touch of the showman, for example, in Gideon's angel who, with a flourish of his walking stick, produces flames that turn Gideon's offering of meat, broth and bread into a burnt sacrifice and then spectacularly disappears (6:21).

Realizing that he had seen an angel disconcerted Gideon so much that we are told he moaned, 'Now I'm going to die!' only to be told by the Lord himself to calm down and stop being silly!

Dear Father, somehow the world feels safer if we think two-dimensionally about the inhabitants of heaven. Do help us to calm down and stop being silly. Maybe we, too, might hear something of importance.

BP

Angels do have wings!

I had a vision of the Lord. He was on his throne high above, and his robe filled the temple. Flaming creatures with six wings each were flying over him. They covered their faces with two of their wings and their bodies with two more. They used the other two wings for flying, as they shouted, 'Holy, holy, holy, Lord All-Powerful! The earth is filled with your glory.'

Now this is more like it. Plenty of wings, worshipful proclamations of faith to the Lord on his throne, flying without wires—super stuff—but why? If it was deemed fit for an angel to take human form to cajole Gideon or save Lot or even accompany the Lord on a visit to Abraham, why the high drama of Isaiah's vision?

My guess is that something dramatic needed to be etched on Isaiah's mind to keep him going through the three reigns that he served the Lord as a prophet, much of this time involving him being the bearer of lousy news to the Israelites.

I think that if I had been picked out to have a flaming winged creature touch my lips with a burning coal, I might have felt that if he asked me to do something for him it would be churlish to refuse.

There is something else important about his encounter. Isaiah is seeing angels in a vision. So, just as John saw the full might and beauty of angels in his Revelation, here Isaiah is being given a glimpse into the throne room of heaven. For anyone worried about being bored in heaven, these peeps of angels 'in the flesh', so to speak, are quite an eye opener, aren't they?

Dear Father, sometimes we envy those who have had a very dramatic Damascus Road experience or claim to have seen angels. Help us to accept that maybe you feel they need the reassurance of an indelible memory like this, either because of events in the past that have damaged their confidence or challenging events that will come in their lives.

BP

Angels are interpreters

'Gabriel, help him understand the vision.'

Angels not only appear in visions, they come alongside us, clearly at the command of God, and help to interpret them, as Daniel discovered here. Also, it is Gabriel, the 'sent one' who appears.

Now Daniel, you remember, was pretty good at interpreting dreams and even the extraordinary writing on the wall in the court of King Balshazzar, but his vision is too complicated even for him. Gabriel explains that it is a positive message from God reassuring his followers that he will finally bring justice to the world and victory for his people. It would seem that God could not risk such an important message being misunderstood.

With Zechariah, God worked differently. He was provided with an angel in human form who 'was there to explain things'—the vision (Zechariah 1:9), but was within the vision itself in order to interpret as he went along—a sort of spiritual simultaneous translation.

In one of the visions, the angel actually asks the Lord to explain it and we are told that the Lord's answer 'was kind and comforting'. This just goes to show that there are no rules about these things and what is important is that we understand what God is saying to us.

Sometimes we, too, have dreams, unexplained pictures and disturbing thoughts. If something is troubling us and we cannot make sense of it, we need to gain confidence that God himself, aware that we are merely human, will be wanting to help us understand. After all, we are told by Jesus that we have recourse to a very special interpreter, superior even to Gabriel. We can call on the Holy Spirit himself.

Dear Father, there are so many times when we cannot understand what it is you are trying to say to us. Help us to remember that even experts of the likes of Daniel needed help in interpreting your messages sometimes. He was not too proud or silly to ask for help. Help us to remember that it is your plan that is important, not our pride.

BP

Angels at births

God sent the angel Gabriel to the town of Nazareth in Galilee with a message for a virgin named Mary.

During this period leading up to the birth of Christ, we sense the same flurry of activity coming backwards and forwards from heaven to earth that we saw at the founding of the Jewish nation. The first sign of it here is the arrival of ace angel Gabriel with news not only for Mary but also for Zechariah.

Both Mary and Zechariah are confused and bothered by the angel's pronouncement that they are to have children and both question Gabriel as to how this can happen. Yet there is clearly a marked difference in their responses. Maybe Zechariah's tone was somewhat dismissive. You can almost see Gabriel drawing himself to his full height (how tall are angels?) before replying. With Mary, however, he could not have been more patient and warm and was rewarded with the famous words, 'I am the Lord's servant! Let it happen as you have said.'

Joseph got a dream angel reassuring him that the baby was not the result of Mary's infidelity. All credit to Joseph that he reacted immediately and married Mary.

It would seem that no one was to be left out of the excitement on the night of Christ's birth. After one chosen angel had passed on God's proud news of Jesus' appearance in the world, the sky was full of them, all singing and glowing and lighting up the heavens like a vast firework display.

Heaven obviously felt that the dream method of angelic visitation was the one for Joseph, though, as they used it again when they wanted to warn him to get Mary and Jesus out of Bethlehem and when it was safe for them to return from Egypt.

What a sigh of relief must have passed through the ranks of angels when they saw Mary and Joseph safely enter Nazareth? A job well done. Time to rest until the next major event.

Dear Father, never let me forget the heavenly excitement that accompanied this seemingly lowly event of Christ's birth.

BP

Deaths, resurrections and ascensions

The angel looked as bright as lightning, and his clothes were white as snow.

Has it ever occurred to you that angels are noticeable by their absence during Jesus' time here on earth? Although mentioned quite frequently by Jesus, they only appear twice—both times in order to comfort their master. The first time was in the desert after his baptism, the second when he is suffering in the garden at Gethsemane. We are told, 'Jesus was in great pain and prayed so sincerely that his sweat fell to the ground like drops of blood'. At this point 'an angel from heaven came to help him', but after this, heaven goes quiet.

No angels are to be seen in the courts of Herod and Pilate or on that hill outside Jerusalem. No angels wipe their master's brow while he is on the cross. Heaven stands helplessly aside while Jesus allows sin and death to envelope him temporarily.

On the third day, however, they are back in action. Rolling away the stone, frightening guards half to death and again bringing gloriously good news. Luke records that, sitting in the empty tomb, two angels ask Mary Magdalene why she is crying, while Mark tells us that the three women visiting the tomb meet a young man who gives them the extraordinary news that Jesus has risen. One thing that all the accounts have in common is that these angels were wearing white (at last!)

A few weeks later, Jesus tells his closest friends that it is time for him to leave them. He lays on another couple of angels, again dressed in white, to reinforce his message after he has gone up to heaven.

Is it allowing our minds to take liberties in imagining the fantastic celebrations in heaven among the angels at the safe return of their Lord and master? I hope not.

Dear Father, thank you for allowing your angels to bring a drop of comfort to your suffering son. Help us to cry out to you in our need and accept your comfort from whomever you provide to minister to us.

BP

Angels in acts

Be sure to welcome strangers into your home. By doing this, some people have welcomed angels as guests, without even knowing it.

The good news for us is that the angels' involvement with earth clearly continues after Jesus goes back to heaven. They continue to pop up when help is needed. They are as dramatic and dynamic as ever with that same single-minded purpose of making sure God's plans are moved forward as they should be. Apostles are released from prison, chains are broken, Philip is pointed in the direction of an Ethiopian official who is hungry to hear how Isaiah's prophecies have been fulfilled. It all has that same stamp of angel authenticity that we see in Genesis and at the beginning of the life of Jesus.

One of my favourite stories is Peter's rescue from prison the night before his trial. I love the idea of Peter being poked awake, told to get dressed and following his appointed angel through threatening, darkened streets, only to be refused entry to his own home by a servant girl who doesn't recognize him in the dark!

Angels still pop up in visions and dreams, too. Perhaps the most crucial one from our point of view is that sent to Cornelius, a Roman centurion. The instructions the angels give him are plain, 'Send some men to Joppa for a man named Simon Peter.' He obeys the command instantly and, when Peter arrives, he recognizes that, if angels can appear to those who are not Jews, then the good news must be for them, too.

We have no reason to suppose that they are not still around, still fighting for us, still working out God's purpose here on earth until that wonderful day when Jesus will return with his holy angels to claim his world. Will we recognize them? Paul tells us that we might entertain them unawares. What an exciting, if frightening, thought.

Dear Father, we so long to see a glimpse of your world, but if seeing angels is not for us, help us to trust that we will see them one day, with you in heaven.

BP

Parties

When she finds it, she calls her friends and neighbours together and says, 'Rejoice with me; I have found my lost coin.'

The great party season is upon us. How do you feel about that? Being a raving introvert at heart, the bigger and livelier the party, the more it saps my energy and makes me want to hibernate somewhere comfortable with a good book. Until way into the New Year, late night fireworks and shouting drunks from other people's parties will disturb my sleep. I hate the extra cooking and food shopping. I'll get fatter. I'll shout into ears of people I hardly know, then fix my face into an inane smile because I can't hear their replies in the hot, overcrowded room.

You can probably tell that I'm not exactly keen on parties. I'd much rather chat with a couple of good friends—though middle-aged partying does beat teenage days where everyone snogged, smoked and/or bopped in time to headache-making music.

Jesus loved parties. If he wasn't going to them, he was talking about them. All three of the 'lost' stories he told—sheep, coin and son—end with a party. It's the same with God in the Old Testament. All those Jerusalem feasts he set up—mega, nationwide parties with best barbequed meat at least thrice yearly. All the dancing he encouraged! The angels can certainly party, too—look what happened when Jesus was born and imagine being the bride at the wedding feast of the Lamb. There will be some parties in heaven!

Many festivities over the next couple of weeks will owe more to the debauched Roman festival of Saturnalia than to anything remotely Christian. However, Christmas is a time to rejoice and celebrate the fact that Jesus came to live on this earth for us and that people still worship him. They do that at Christmas more than at any other time of year.

Whether you're a party-lover or hate them, invite Jesus into your social life, including any parties you're going to this year.

CL

Self-pity

'Yet you never even gave me a young goat so I could celebrate with my friends.'

Today is my birthday. Unfortunately, it occurs on the same silly date every year. Although I'm not into parties, it would be nice to go out for a pub lunch with a couple of friends, but they're all like me—far too stressed, rushing round in circles, getting ready for Christmas. Anyway, all the local eateries are serving dried-up turkey to boozy office workers, accompanied by muzak dreams of a white Christmas that make me grind my teeth. The skies are grey, the ground muddy and people keep saying they're going down with the flu. Eeyore becomes my role model. No, Eeyore enjoyed being miserable and made his friends smile. Usually, in our house, some innocent bystander gets an earful.

Self-pity—it's so pathetic. I have so much to enjoy—including friends and family who love me. I could be full of thankfulness, but I'm like the whining older son in Jesus' story. He was always with his father. Everything his father had was his, yet he couldn't enter into the joy and celebration when his brother, who had lost all this, was found again.

My self-pitying gloom centres on a trivial issue, but Christmas is a truly difficult season for many people. Everyone is 'supposed' to be having a wonderful time, but for those who have suffered loss, all the parties and fun can rub salt in raw wounds. I guess, though, anyone who, with God's help, resists resentment at others' joy and then finds something to celebrate—Jesus' birth, for example—will be walking in God's ways and may even feel better, too!

Lord, you have pity on us always, so there's no need for us to wallow in miserable self-pity, even if there is a good reason. Help those who, for whatever reason, struggle with parties and celebrations this year. Encourage each of us with glimpses of the Father's joy and celebration as we celebrate his son's birthday.

CL

Best wine for the party

Nearby stood six stone water jars, the kind used by the Jews for ceremonial washing, each holding from twenty to thirty gallons.

You know how toddlers love being whooshed through the air and tipped upside down? I find that, surprisingly often, reading the Bible has a similar effect. Well, Jesus did say we have to be like little children to enter his kingdom...

At a village wedding, Jesus makes about 150 gallons of vintage Château Bar-Joseph. How many people would have been at the party—surely not more than 300? That's half a gallon, or over two litres, each—and they'd already drunk the original intoxicants dry. How outrageous, tipping my 'correct Christian morality' upside down! Both Old and New Testaments contain plenty of evidence that God hates drunkenness. What was Jesus doing?

John says that Jesus was doing the first of his miraculous signs, revealing his glory so that the disciples put their faith in him. Cynics might say, 'Young men would follow a guy who performed this kind of party trick!' but more is going on here. Jesus turned 150 gallons of water for Jewish ceremonial washing (imagine carting that from the well!) into the intoxicating wine of the gospel. It reminds me of Peter having to explain on the Jewish feast of Pentecost, 'These men are not drunk, as you suppose. It's only nine in the morning!' (Acts 2:15).

This 'sign' shows us a lot about Jesus—and his Father. Not the kind of God who spoils the party by telling the kids to wash their hands all the time, instead he enhances celebrations, transforming them from black and white to Technicolor. His generosity runs to extravagance—especially towards people who are poor and oppressed—and he is surprising. We're not following a set of rules, we're following a wonderful God-man. He whooshes his children to the moon and back quite safely while they chuckle and ask for more.

Read Ephesians 5:18. Ask God to help you stay child-like this Christmas—and drunk, on the Holy Spirit, of course!

CL

Costly party

The Son of Man came eating and drinking, and you say, 'Here is a glutton and a drunkard, a friend of tax collectors and "sinners".'

A water-into-wine party piece could sound cheap—and someone has to pay the price for the kind of superabundant grace we were thinking about yesterday. John the Baptist was in prison when he sent to ask his cousin, Jesus, 'Are you the one who is to come or should we expect someone else?' John's mission, understood almost from the womb, was to prepare the way for the Messiah by urging people to repent and be baptized. Not a party-lover but an ascetic prophet, first living the desert, then imprisoned for doing God's work, John paid a huge price—his life, finally. However, it wasn't enough. Jesus said that none born of women was greater than John, 'yet the one who is least in the kingdom of God is greater than he'. He also remarked that John, 'came neither eating bread nor drinking wine, and you say, "He has a demon."'

Cousin Jesus, by contrast, was accused of partying, eating and drinking too much, mixing with sinful people who lived it up. He reached many, but that wasn't quite enough either.

Today, we kingdom people who are 'greater than John the Baptist' (!) regularly drink wine together. It signifies the blood of one who loved to mix with sinners but was himself entirely free from sin. As we swallow that wine, it's as though we are allowing the pure life of Jesus to flow within us. He lived life to the full. Our intoxication with the Holy Spirit is only possible because of his amazing sacrifice. His miracle grace is anything but cheap.

He calls us to take up our cross and follow him. Following him means partying with and befriending sinners, which may well be harder spiritually than joining a desert nunnery.

Jesus, thank you for mixing with and then dying for us sinners, that we might enjoy knowing you and experience your holy life—life in all its fullness.

CL

Party behaviour

He was being carefully watched...

People-watching at parties can be fun. Some very religious people watched Jesus at a party meal. Hardly the politest of guests, he waded straight in, challenging deeply held beliefs with direct questions and action. Talk about causing social embarrassment! I imagine that the guest who was healed of dropsy (where watery fluid collects in the body's cavities or tissues) enjoyed the best party ever—after he was 'sent away'. Sadly, the prominent Pharisee host couldn't rejoice with him. The atmosphere at his party must have become decidedly strained, especially as Jesus, having done some people-watching of his own, offered unasked-for advice that overturned what were deemed to be the correct standards of Pharisaic etiquette, pouring shame on host and guests alike.

Pharisees strove to obey the rules of God and man, doing everything decently and in order. At a party meal, they would make sure that they gave people the correct places of honour. Jesus upset the carefully worked-out seating plan by advising everyone to take the lowest place. Imagine the chaos that would cause! Then he informed his host that he'd invited the wrong kind of people anyway. If he wanted God's reward, why ask respectable folk who would invite him back? He should have filled the place with outcasts—the poor, crippled, lame and blind—those less than perfect who were normally pushed to, or over, the edge of Jewish religious and social life.

This story raises the uncomfortable question, what kind of people do we invite to meals or parties? I know we see the word 'Pharisee' and read 'baddie', but I feel some sympathy here and wonder, had I been hostess that day, might I have begun to consider Jesus to be the guest to dread?

Thank you, Jesus, that you love all people so much. I want to follow your heart, rather than social, cultural or religious rules. Where I'm blind, show me. In particular, show me exactly who to include in the warmth of your love over this Christmas season.

CL

Party invitations

Go out into the roads and country lanes and make them come in.

I wonder in what tone of voice his fellow guest responded to Jesus' words that those who invite outcasts to their banquet will be blessed and repaid at the resurrection of the righteous? 'Blessed is the man who will eat at the feast in the kingdom of God.' Was his tone longing (if only I could be there) or sanctimonious (as a son of Abraham, I'm home and dry, mate)?

Whichever one it was, he did not understand that Jesus had made God's kingdom present as well as future. The Father gave the world the biggest gift, the biggest party ever, in sending Jesus. However, many who claimed to be God's chosen ones weren't accepting the gift or the invitation. Their excuses varied from 'I'm too busy or important' to 'It's wrong to heal on the Sabbath'. So, in telling the parable of the great banquet, I wonder if Jesus' tone was angry.

I'm not sure God ever does *make* anyone come to his party. However, people do need someone to go proactively, to explain who exactly has invited them—and impact them with the truth that they are more than welcome. It hurts us, too, when, as 'beggars showing other beggars where to find bread' at his table, rich or poor ones turn away, but we never know. 'Did I once sit next to you at a Chamber of Commerce dinner, Chris?' a shop-owner asked me when he learnt which road and church I used to inhabit. I'd never been to such a dinner; it must have been my former next-door neighbour, Carrie, over 15 years ago. 'I've been a Christian just three years—but it all began with that conversation,' he explained. When I phoned Carrie she said, 'Oh Chris, I never feel I do anything much!'

We'll meet many people in the next few days, Lord—friends, harassed sales staff, family members who annoy or appal us. Enable us to be your invitation-bearers.

CL

Christmas praise party

Sing to the Lord a new song, his praise in the assembly of the saints.

The Old Testament praise party described in this psalm sounds exuberant—singing, dancing, tambourine, harp... Under the new covenant, we can celebrate even more! On Christmas day, we open the presents, but it's Jesus' birthday party. When our children were little, we used to sing 'Happy birthday to Jesus' as a family. It's an old, familiar song—as so many of our Christmas carols are. ('Carol' means 'dance'.) I guess God doesn't become as tired of hearing carols and other praise songs as I imagine British royalty must do of musical pleas to 'Save the Queen'. Whatever the case, why not let your hair down and celebrate by singing Jesus a new song today, by yourself on your bed or with other partying Christians in joyful assembly?

All this happy-clappy praise partying—isn't it about as enduring and useful as the bubbles in a glass of Christmas champagne? These days my grown-up son demands to know what kind of a god wants people praising him morning, noon and night? They are fair questions—and maybe this psalm contains part of an answer. Maybe heartfelt praise is a weapon of our spiritual warfare. That's easy to see on a personal level because it's hard to really praise God while maintaining a blinkered, selfish perspective or other bad attitude. As we praise him, our hope and faith rises. Despite the sad or terrible things that we may see around, we are declaring that we know he is Lord, he is good, he loves, he acts, he crowns the humble with salvation, he even takes delight in us! Remember that, whether you're rushing about feeding what feels like 5000 or struggling with loneliness, alone or in a crowd.

Read the new song that poured from Mary's mouth when she shared with her cousin the amazing news that she was bearing God's child (Luke 1:46–55). Enter into her joy and let your own spill out—for he still does lift up the humble and fills the hungry with good things.

CL

Party politics

So the king and Haman went to dine with Queen Esther, and as they were drinking wine on that second day the king again asked, 'Queen Esther, what is your petition?'

Not all parties in the Bible are given for lame ducks. Here, Esther is entertaining despotic King Xerxes and his scheming henchman, Haman. True, the king is her husband, but she's no longer his favourite wife and one word from him could spell her death. She's also Jewish—her ancestors were carried into exile and her people are now subjects of Xerxes' vast kingdom, which comprises '127 provinces stretching from India to Cush' (1:1). Haman's machinations mean that her people are under a death sentence. Feeling totally inadequate, Esther finds that she is the only person who might save them. Her uncle asks, 'Who knows but that you have come to royal position for such a time as this?' A brave woman, Esther uses the weapons at her disposal—her best dress and two fine banquets—to play 'party' politics, save her people and ensure that Haman meets the fate he deserves.

I hope that your entertaining over the festive season will be in less dramatic circumstances, but it could still be strategic in terms of God's purposes. If you have guests and are feeling that you might as well be a potato-peeling machine or chamber maid, remember that some have entertained angels unawares. Think of Mary and Martha who provided a home from home for Jesus and his friends or the two women who did the same for Elisha (2 Kings 4). Those who gave hospitality to the 72 disciples Jesus sent out in pairs were healed and welcomed into God's kingdom. If you're a guest, perhaps travelling a distance with fretful children, pray that peace will be on the house where you're staying.

Being hospitable demands skill, tact and hard work. Being a guest isn't always easy, but God cares about both! Invite him to use the hospitality you're offering—and/or your experience of being a guest —during this festive season.

CL

Immoral parties

Woe to those who are heroes at drinking wine and champions at mixing drinks, who acquit the guilty for a bribe, but deny justice to the innocent.

Wine is good—here God is seen as vineyard tender and winemaker and we know that he loves parties. Good gifts can be twisted and abused, though. They certainly were in the eighth century BC when Isaiah was writing. People called good evil and evil good: 'Getting drunk is great—who cares about justice, truth or the poor?' Isaiah's words sound distressingly familiar in the 21st century AD where a good night out for many is a binge-drinking session, following which the 'weak' need their stomachs pumped and the 'strong' get into fights. Those who don't join in the more extreme clubbing/party scene are seen as weirdo killjoys or, at best, ignorant.

'Don't knock it till you've tried it!' I've been told by young adults. Well, I'm sorry, I wouldn't enjoy the vomiting, hangovers, crude, aggressive side of personalities coming to the fore and damage, either creeping or sudden. This isn't light, it's darkness. It isn't sweet, but bitter. It was bad enough when I was a teenager, but what with drugs and 'ladettes' outdoing 'laddish culture', it's worse now. Please pray for 'Generation X'.

God said, 'Woe to those who rise early in the morning to run after their drinks, who stay up late at night till they are inflamed by wine.' Massive woe does come to alcoholics and to those who love them. 'They have harps and lyres at their banquets, tambourines and flute and wine' (or electric guitars, sound systems and drugs) 'but they have no regard for the deeds of the Lord, no respect for the work of his hands.' No respect for the people he made or even for their own bodies. If we're not in awe of our creator God, unhealthy, evil things can so easily fill the gap.

Pray for the empty ones this party season. Pray especially for those who habitually abuse alcohol and/or drugs—and for those who love them.

CL

Parties when you're hurting

Why do the wicked... make merry to the sound of the flute... spend their years in prosperity and go down to the grave in peace.

This is such a difficult time of year for many people. Friends may be away with their families. The normal routine usually stops for a week or so while everyone is supposedly enjoying themselves. There must be plenty who want to throw something at the jolly togetherness splurging from their TV screens—those who are bereaved or divorced, singles stuck caring for infirm parents, those who are ill or in some kind of institution, even those in a foreign country far from home.

We've read Isaiah where he's railing against immoral parties, but the people Job describes don't sound especially wicked: 'Their homes are safe and free from fear... their little ones dance about.' Their parties appear fine—not at all like drunken orgies—but Job has lost all his family, health and possessions. When he sees other people enjoying themselves, it rankles. Surely, it's unfair—these people don't want to know God and yet all is well with them, whereas Job tried his best to know and serve God and look what happened!

Yes, life is unfair; some of the best people suffer the most terrible calamities. We can spend forever trying to work out why, but we do know that, whatever individuals are going through, God longs to be with them—comforting those who mourn, weeping with those who weep, befriending the lonely, strengthening the weak. He needs us sometimes—to be his arms giving people a hug, doing their shopping or sitting with them in silence, during this Christmas season and also through the months to come.

Lord, we pray for all who for various sad reasons aren't going to enjoy the festivities this year. Help us to be sensitive and remember those we can draw alongside with tenderness, as you yourself do. Help us to comfort others with the comfort you have given us.

CL

Good reason to party!

Then he went with them into the temple courts, walking and jumping, and praising God.

Some terrible scenes had happened in the temple courts not long before. A furious Jesus saw callous traders exploiting poor worshippers and violently cleansed what should have been sacred space. Then he was tried in the court of the high priest while, outside, Peter disowned him three times.

Jesus, who brought healing and new life to so many; Jesus whom many believed to be the Messiah who would rescue them from the hated Roman occupiers, was condemned to death, then crucified. Now a beggar, aged over 40, who isn't allowed into the temple because he's been disabled from birth, is healed instantly in Jesus' name by Peter of all people! No wonder the former beggar is having his own personal praise party, leaping and shouting all over the temple. He's never had anything to celebrate before. No wonder, too, that people are running to see him—and staying to hear more about this Jesus who still saves and heals people even though he died. They don't understand yet that Jesus rose from the grave and ascended into heaven, but they do understand that this man who has sat begging at the Beautiful Gate for so many years is bouncing around like a six-year-old.

Who knows why sometimes God is with us, drawing alongside, bringing comfort but not removing our distress and why, at other times, he works a miracle and turns someone's mourning or sickness literally into dancing? All we know here is that, after this miracle, 'the number of men' (who believed) 'grew to about 5000' (4:4). Before that, 3000 had been saved at Pentecost and others were 'added daily', but this particular miracle caused enough of a stir to worry the religious authorities deeply.

Let's pray for miracles that will draw people's attention to the fact that Jesus lives and cares and loves people today. When they happen, never mind New Year or anyone's birthday, let's really party!

CL

Ongoing party

Every day they continued to meet together in the temple courts. They broke bread in their homes and ate together with glad and sincere hearts, praising God and enjoying the favour of all the people.

OK, we've just gone backwards in Acts, but it seems to me that the baby Church, which formed after the 3000 were saved at Pentecost, enjoyed an ongoing party. It may have been quieter than the beggar who jumped and praised God, but it was the best kind of party. The new Christians were 'together'. They had 'everything in common'. Some parties are designed to show off wealth, but in this one they sold what they had and gave to anyone in need.

I saw a couple on breakfast television today. Having won £7.6 million at Lotto, they spent some on themselves, but gave a considerable amount to family and charities. 'What's the point having money festering in a bank when it could be doing good?' the couple said. 'Giving it away and seeing the good it does makes us really happy.' The TV presenters seemed amazed, but delighted with them. 'What lovely people!' they said.

Parties don't have to be elaborate. Meeting together is all you need for a great party. Sharing bread in each other's homes is more than enough. Caring for each other and anyone in need, concentrating on giving not getting, will make any party special. Praising God together with glad and sincere hearts guarantees a great party. The new Christians had reason to be glad—not only was Jesus alive but also miracles were being done by apostles who, until a few days before, had been hiding away, useless, frightened. The Holy Spirit transformed them into bold ambassadors for Jesus. He gave them, not the Dutch courage of alcohol, but something far more amazing that meant Peter had to explain, 'These men are not drunk as you suppose. It's only nine in the morning!' (Acts 2:15).

Thank you, Lord, that, while there are people following you, there's no reason for your amazing party to stop!

CL

Wedding party

'Blessed are those who are invited to the wedding supper of the Lamb!'

Will you be seeing the New Year in tonight, either at home or at a party? Personally I fail to see what is so exciting about 2004 becoming 2005. I'd rather not sing the unintelligible words of Auld Lang Syne, dodging the debris of party poppers while my feet are trampled by tipsy strangers. I prefer to fall asleep well before midnight if fireworks and revellers allow. A wedding, though, now that is something to dress up for, celebrate, cheer about, weep tears of joy over—especially a wedding where you are the bride!

After all, what's a New Year, when time itself will be made new? There will be new heavens, a new earth and a new dress for the bride, of 'fine linen, bright and clear'. Forget New Year resolutions, you'll be given clothes of righteousness. Forget careful make-up and hairdos or the fact that you're feeling a year older—you'll become 'radiant', 'without stain or wrinkle or any other blemish' (Ephesians 5:27). Forget yourself and remember who it is that you are going to marry! For you are part of the Church universal, who is Christ's beloved bride. It's way beyond the capacity of our thoughts or imagination, this wedding supper of the Lamb, but we know that it's been devised by our Father—our creator God—who loves us and his son. Not a quiet affair, the noise that the multitude of heavenly and earthly beings make will sound 'like the roar of rushing waters and like loud peals of thunder'. It takes place in the heaven they made together for us all to enjoy and you and I are invited. It's going to be some party!

Enjoy your party tonight or your quiet night in but, if you keep on living with this wedding party in your heart, it will transform your life!

Father, thank you for making a place just for me at your son's wedding feast. Let that hope surge through my life like champagne bubbles throughout the coming year.

CL

DAY BY DAY WITH GOD

MAGAZINE SECTION

Great truths children have learned

Christine Platt

You can't hide a piece of broccoli in a glass of milk! Sooner or later someone—probably Mum—is going to notice that dark green floret floating gently in its creamy pool. To a child, a glass of milk looks to be a fantastic hiding place for the unwanted veggie, until experience shows that it doesn't disappear or glide obediently to the bottom, but keeps bobbing up, however much you try to push it down!

To a teacher this would be a lesson in physics, thus vital for the child's education: some things float; some things sink. From my scant memories of school physics lessons, it has something to do with density. To a parent, however, there would be a more moral application. The child was endeavouring to deceive... to make it look as though she had eaten the broccoli, whereas she had actually hidden it.

The source of deception

Deception has its roots right at the beginning of human history. Eve's first recorded words to God were, 'The serpent deceived me and I ate' (Genesis 3:13). She blamed the serpent for deceiving her as she attempted to justify herself before God. She and Adam then tried to deceive God himself by hiding in the garden. They were hoping to avoid facing up to their wrongdoing. We bear the legacy of that first deception. The urge to lie, to give false impressions, to cheat and to exaggerate has been with us ever since.

We only have to look around us and see the misery this causes in individual lives, families, workplaces and nations—men and women being unfaithful to their marriage vows, workers fiddling their expenses, media spin, fraud and corruption, Hitler managing to convince some Western governments that he could be trusted not to invade other nations. In small ways and large, deception is a human characteristic.

The outworking of deceit

As we mature, we move on from hiding our broccoli to more sophisticated deceptions. Some people go to extremes to hide the ageing process, with face lifts, tummy tucks and hair implants. The lie that's been propagated is, 'Youth is the be all and end all—from thirty onwards it's all downhill!' Caring for our bodies and presenting ourselves as well as possible is really important, and the old saying is true: 'Any old barn door looks better for a coat of paint'! But taken to extremes, the quest for youthfulness is desperately sad. 'Mutton dressed as lamb' comes to mind. We've all been young and we're all going to grow old. It's a complete waste of time, money and energy to aim for eternal youth—a philosophy based on deceit. We need to be authentic at each stage of life's journey.

Broccoli won't sink!

Some initial deception is sometimes necessary in order to get on with others. We've all met people who are tiresome and boring. When someone offends us, we often need to hide our anger and hurt behind a nice polite smile. Unfortunately emotions, like broccoli, keep bobbing up. Volcanoes look the epitome of rocklike stability on the outside but the boiling turmoil within is suddenly revealed when they explode.

Unresolved anger can only be contained for so long. It will erupt in time. If you keep putting more and more broccoli into a glass of milk, the milk will eventually overflow. We need to deal with each piece of broccoli before we reach danger point and run the risk of harming others. 'See to it that no one misses the grace of God and that no bitter root grows up to cause trouble and defile many' (Hebrews 12:15).

Hurts need to be faced and brought to God. He is the only safe place to bring our anger and churning emotions. Friends can also help, but our first port of call needs to be God. He can enable us to forgive those who have hurt us. It's easy to write that, but I'm sure we've all heard people say, 'I could never forgive that person for what they've done. I've tried, but I can't.' Their anger is palpable and quite often justified. They have been deeply wronged. Our hearts go out to them and we think, 'In their shoes I'd find it hard to forgive too.'

Corrie ten Boom is a constant inspiration to me in this area of forgiveness. She was a Dutch woman whose family helped Jews escape in World War II. She was imprisoned in the horror of a concentration camp where her father and sister both died. By an error (or God's sovereign plan!) she was released and began sharing her experiences with others all around the world. One of her themes was forgiveness. One day, after she had spoken, a man with a broad smile approached her and said, 'I'm so glad to hear you speak today. I was a guard at your camp and I've become a Christian. Will you forgive me?' Corrie was flooded with ghastly memories and knew that in herself she was incapable of forgiving this man who had so tormented her and her family. She cried out to God and asked him to pour his forgiveness into her at that moment. God answered and Corrie was enabled to reach out and embrace this man who had so profoundly wounded her.

God never deceives

What a relief to read of Jesus, the one perfect human being: 'He committed no sin, and no deceit was found in his mouth' (1 Peter 2:22). With Jesus, what you saw was what you got. He was totally honest.

I often wonder why I find it so hard to trust God's promises fully. He has always been faithful in the past. Why do I doubt that he will be faithful in the future? Maybe this endemic deceitfulness has so marked my soul that I can't quite believe anyone, even God, could be genuine.

In the Bible, God's constant refrain to his people is 'Remember…' Remember how I rescued you. Remember how I provided for you. Remember how I led you. Remember how I protected you. Remember what I taught you. Remember what happened last time and apply it to this situation. God will never deceive us. He will always remain true to his character and his word.

When the psalmist was in trouble and doubting God, he said to himself, 'I will remember the deeds of the Lord; yes, I will remember your miracles of long ago. I will meditate on all your works and consider all your mighty deeds' (Psalm 77:11, 12). He started the psalm in the depths of despair and finished full of praise and confidence in God, just because he *remembered*.

Self-deception

Another aspect God wants us to be clear about is in 1 John 1:8: 'If we claim to be without sin, we deceive ourselves and the truth is not in us.' A wise saying I heard recently is, 'The worst lies are not the ones we tell others but the ones we tell ourselves and end up believing.'

Some of us avoid looking at the sin within ourselves. We try to hide all sorts of veggies in our milk, but God is not fooled, and most people aren't either. King David of Israel got it right when he said, 'Surely you desire truth in the inner parts' (Psalm 51:6). With God we can be utterly honest, utterly ourselves—no masks, no trying to be what we are not, no deception. This is true freedom.

Maybe some of us can't even see the broccoli any more. We don't realize the extent to which sin has warped our minds, attitudes and actions. I often use this prayer of David: 'Search me, O God, and know my heart, test me and know my anxious thoughts. See if there is any offensive way in me, and lead me in the way everlasting' (Psalm 139:23–24). This gives God permission gently to expose areas of our lives where he wants to bring about change and renewal.

God forgives and heals

Asking God to put his searchlight on our lives can be a scary prospect. What horrid things are lurking in dark corners? The liberating news is that nothing is hidden from God. He is saddened by our sin, but not shocked by it. Humanity's propensity for evil holds no surprises for him. He has witnessed all of human history—murder, rape, brutality, lies, torture, injustice. He watched as his only Son was murdered. There is nothing in my heart or yours too awful for him to deal with. When his holy fire blazes into our lives and reveals sin, his desire is not to destroy but to cleanse and restore.

God explains this through Isaiah the prophet: 'Ah, sinful nation, a people loaded with guilt... Come now, let us reason together, says the Lord. Though your sins are like scarlet, they shall be white as snow; though they are red as crimson, they shall be like wool' (Isaiah 1:4, 18). He is in the business of transforming lives, but he can't do it unless we invite him to do his holy work. Facing up to sin hurts. No one likes to admit they've blown it. But the relief of forgiveness and the experience of wholeness are worth all the pain. This is part of the abundant life he offers. Milk tastes much better without broccoli in it!

Let's invite him to do his renewing work in us. 'If we walk in the light, as he is in the light, we have fellowship with one another, and the blood of Jesus, his Son, purifies us from all sin' (I John 1:7).

An extract from *The Art of Waiting*

The Art of Waiting *is BRF's 2004 Advent book. It explores the theme of waiting that characterizes this season of the Church's year as well as being something that is part of everybody's daily life—from waiting for a kettle to boil to expecting a phone call that might bring bad news. Author Wendy Bray shows how we can discover God using all kinds of 'waiting times' to draw us closer to himself. This is Wendy's second book for BRF, following* In the Palm of God's Hand *(2000), which described her experience of cancer.*

Gallery: 'The Crowd in Waiting'

Before you is a wide, expansive canvas, the first of a pair. You have glimpsed its twin in the distance, further along the gallery. But for now your breath is taken away by the magnificence of this first painting, and most specifically by its glorious riot of colour, shape and texture.

That colour, rich and intense at the bottom, fades to a brilliant dizzying golden light at the very top, drawing your eye ever upwards. You wonder at the imagination and creativity behind this tapestry of hue, this glorious jewelled embroidery of light and tone, depth and surface, shadow and light, boldness and fragility. The colour may be rich, even eccentric, but the paint has been skilfully applied in painstaking detail.

You step back in an attempt to take in not just the size and scope of the painting, but the figures portrayed, for it shows you a crowd of humanity…

There are people from all walks of life, all ages of time, all professions, all trades, all nations. There is a medieval farmer with his plough, a black jazz musician apparently soulfully struggling to make his instrument heard, an office worker with an overflowing in-tray. Children are chasing here and there, round and between the legs of parents. Babies reach out for their mothers, young women blush at the sight of young men. A footballer celebrates the scoring of a goal with an upward leap, his fist punching the air. A cook tastes a spoonful of the ingredients he is preparing in a large mixing bowl, while an opera singer curtsies to receive a flamboyant bouquet. To one side, shunned by most of the passing crowd, a beggar holds out his hand in supplication, his clothes torn and muddied, an ugly scar across his forehead.

A clergyman is marrying a blushing bride and a nervously hunched groom. Two men are building a wall, one bending for the mortar, the other lifting a pile of new bricks. A woman stands weeping, her hands pressed to her tear-stained cheeks, alone, even in such a crowd. Youths wander apparently aimlessly, with scowls on their faces and their hands deep in their pockets. Two businessmen are shaking on a deal; bulging briefcases at their feet.

You see aggression and tenderness, intention and regret, work and play all portrayed here. You cannot imagine how many weeks and months the painter took to achieve such detail. What vision kept him at his canvas through day and night? It is as if he knows each one portrayed, wonderfully capturing the fears and frustrations, needs, joys and hidden gifts of each personality. The dreams they dream, the plans they have made, the hope and disappointment they carry, have somehow been made visible.

You look again to see a woman. A shawl is pulled around her shoulders, a tiny child is held close and she is looking into the far distance, anxiety furrowing her brow. Beyond her gaze, two trapeze artists swing from a highwire above, frozen in mid-air and in time. On a high shelf to one side, a beautiful clock sits in full view of the crowd. A few faces are lifted towards it, expectant, as if waiting for it to chime or to watch its hands move into place.

This is the busyness, the bustle, the beautiful ordinariness and tragic tenderness that is life. But there is a paradox in this painting. Despite the hectic pace of life portrayed, the hum of activity, the purpose and intention, the 'going everywhere fast' that is set before you, there is a sense of going nowhere slowly—of being stuck on the down escalator of life when you were expecting to go up.

Looking closer, you notice that in the midst of it all there is a sense of frustrated expectancy, a 'not yet' on the breeze, a call for patience. There is a hesitancy that you can't quite place despite the boldness of the brushwork.

Then you begin to understand the artist's intention. This is a waiting crowd—waiting not for something to be shared or for a play to start, but for a word, a word that will set them free from the frenetic pace they have set themselves, a word that will dry their tears, ease their pain and restore their sight. A word which will tell them that they can indeed pass beyond this place, that their wait is over, that it is 'time'.

And then you locate the hidden essence of that word in a face or two. It is etched into the weary lines, the tired eyes. It is hope...

Paul and a longed-for birth

The creation waits in eager expectation for the sons of God to be revealed. For the creation was subjected to frustration, not by its own choice, but by the will of the one who subjected it, in hope that the creation itself will be liberated from its bondage to decay and brought into the glorious freedom of the children of God. We know that the whole creation has been groaning as in the pains of childbirth right up to the present time. Not only so, but we ourselves, who have the firstfruits of the spirit, groan inwardly as we wait eagerly for our adoption as sons, the redemption of our bodies. For in this hope we were saved. But hope that is seen is no hope at all. Who hopes for what he already has? But if we hope for what we do not yet have, we wait for it patiently.

Romans 8:19–25

These verses really are a song of Advent waiting. They are the ongoing anthem of creation and the ballad of salvation rolled into one, with the yearning of a love song.

Creation is waiting, Paul explains, because God has put the brakes on, held it up, made it wait—but for a glorious purpose. It is his plan that instead of sinking into bondage and decay, creation can be liberated.

God the creator just loves his creation. (Remember, in Genesis

1:31, 'God saw all that he had made, and it was very good.') He wants to see it restored in all its glory, in a glorious all-encompassing relationship with him—new heavens and a new earth. First and foremost, that includes our relationship with him as father, so Paul uses a very human illustration to make his point.

It may seem strange for Paul, not known for his feminine sympathies, to portray creation in waiting in such a maternal way. Even Paul must have known that when he was speaking of a new life longed for and laboured for, he could hardly escape the birth illustration. There is something familiar, yet exciting in the way that such a commonplace—but none the less miraculous—event as the birth of a child is used to assure us of the even more exciting eventuality God has planned for us. Even those who do not or cannot know the experience of expecting a child or the enjoyment of a relationship with a parent can know this hope as God-given. We do not need to have previously experienced family life to enjoy a perfect relationship with our Father God—the most natural and fulfilling relationship of all.

A friend of mine, a counsellor and social worker who often leads seminars on family and adoption issues, tells the wonderful story of waiting for his first child. He and his wife had been hoping for a baby for some years, but after numerous medical tests and consultations it became apparent that they would not be able to have a child of their own.

After much heart-searching, they decided to apply for adoption, hoping to give their love and care to a baby who could become their own. They had never-ending paperwork to complete, difficult and stressful interviews and assessments to face, and a long and agonizing wait. It often seemed that they would never have the child they longed for. Then they were asked to visit a baby boy in foster care with a view to adoption. It was love at first sight, at least for my friend's wife—my friend took a little longer! But through, or despite, the nappies and wet kisses, this needy little boy reached my friend's heart.

They returned home full of hope, but within a few days complications arose that cast doubt over whether this baby could be the one to start their family. Another anxious wait followed, many tears, and some desperation. Then one morning my friend received a telephone call in the middle of a seminar. It was his wife. She had heard from the adoption agency: the little boy could be theirs.

My friend says he remembers that day as if it was yesterday, despite the fact that his 'little boy' has just left university. There are many times when he looks at his tall, energetic son and remembers the wait for him, the call that made it all worthwhile, and the moment when he officially became a dad. He had waited patiently for a relationship he had only ever been able to long for. The small baby who became a strapping son is a constant reminder of hope fulfilled.

How does it feel to wait and hope for 'what is unseen' (2 Corinthians 4:18)? It is something like the deep yearning that envelops us when we long for a child, the ache of longing that joins two lovers who are far apart and the homesickness for hills and fields when we are confined to city streets. Through such experiences, God can plant a seed in our hearts that grows into a longing for him, a hope of relationship with him, and a hope for all he has prepared for us. It's just that often we don't recognize it as such, and live believing that it is the things 'seen' that will fill the gap, ease the longing, meet the need. They don't, of course. Our greatest need is for God.

Our greatest hope is for the unseen that God has promised us—our eternal life with the one who loves us more than we can ever imagine. For that, as Paul says, we must wait patiently. And expect some groaning along the way!

Reflect...
What am I really waiting for?

Father, patience is not my virtue; waiting is not my favourite game. But a plan like yours needs time to reach perfection, time to touch hearts, time to reach the lost. As I wait for what I do not have, give me hope.

To order a copy of this book, turn to page 157.

An extract from *Why Siblings Matter*

This book examines the importance of sibling relationships—links that can strengthen families as much as the vertical, parent–child bonds. They may shape our lives from birth to late teens, as well as having an impact in the wider family of the church. Why Siblings Matter *explores seven areas of vulnerability for such relationships as well as the biblical principles that can help. Author Anna Brooker is an ordained Church of England minister, with nearly twenty years' previous teaching experience in primary schools, specializing in working with special needs children.*

Second helpings: The new dynamics of sibling relationships

As we looked up at the life-sized photo on the wall, both the words and the image of two children in a park conveyed a deeply reassuring message. It conveyed the importance of friendship and trust between children, which can first be learned in the family, with their siblings. Children's stories and adult novels frequently focus on the benefits of strong sibling relationships, and the dangers of poor ones, from Jane Austen and George Eliot to Enid Blyton and Arthur Ransome, to many excellent contemporary children's stories by authors such as Jaqueline Wilson. Even in fairy tales, the theme is evident: Hansel and Gretel help and comfort each other, whereas Cinderella's sisters' ugliness is the outward sign of, and maybe even the punishment for, their unkind treatment of her. In fairy tales, after all, the good are invariably beautiful and the bad are ugly…

Love–hate

There are two universal assumptions about siblings: they will love each other… and they will hate each other. The paradox is that both are true, for the archetypal love–hate relationship is the one between siblings. This has been well documented by Adele Faber and Elaine Mazlish in their fascinating book, *Siblings without Rivalry*, which makes compulsive reading for parents. They describe two forces at work—one pushing the siblings apart as they use the differences between them to establish themselves as unique individuals, the other drawing them together into their unique bond as siblings. All parents of two or more children watch this paradox being played out every day as siblings fight one minute, hug the next; or disagree violently at lunchtime but laugh together uproariously over supper. Brothers and sisters really bring out the best and the worst in each other: they know 'which buttons to push' to annoy each other, but equally, they can offer each other unconditional sympathy and com-fort like no one else can. As one mother of two put it, 'Their fighting is exhausting—but when the chips are down they can be sweet to each other… helpful and supportive.'

Interestingly, in his letter to the Romans, Paul describes not just interpersonal relationships, but the whole human condition, in terms of an inward struggle between the forces of good and evil: 'Even when I want to do right, I cannot. Instead of doing what I know is right, I do wrong' (Romans 7:18–19).

Paul's description takes us to the very heart of sibling relationships, for they are intrinsically linked to the personal, inward battle to conquer our self-centredness and insecurities that faces every human being. Winning the battle is crucial, for the family as a whole, for every individual within it, and for all their future relationships. We need to remember that just as positive family relationships create the environment in which security, love and trust can grow, the very closeness of those same relationships makes them the breeding ground for insecurity, jealousy and hatred.

So let's look now at how the behaviour of adults can strengthen or weaken sibling relationships…

One to one

Each child needs the undivided attention of his or her parents on a regular basis. We will never get to know and understand our children well unless we spend time with them on their own as well as with the rest of the family. In addition, rivalry for parental attention, which often leads to sibling conflict, can be stopped only through giving each child one-to-one time. One father highlighted the need to spend time 'every day with each of them', and later told me how, as a child in a large family, he had only really felt 'equally loved' at bedtime, when his parents said prayers with each child on their own. Another father pointed out the challenge of being there for each child, particularly when, as in his case, the age gaps are quite large: 'You need to work at spending as much time with the youngest as you did with the older ones, which isn't easy as you get older, busier, less interested, etc.'

It's good to bear in mind, however, that we don't need to be doing anything particularly special for our children to benefit. In fact, I heard a preacher once talk about his young children all eagerly volunteering, the minute he said the immortal words, 'Would one of you like to come…?' Long before he'd finished saying where he was going, they sensed the chance of some one-to-one time with him. It may be a walk to nursery, to the postbox, to the shops or park, or reading a story, or doing a jigsaw together—anything, in fact, where the child knows that they have you to themselves, without interruption, for a few minutes. One of my most lasting memories of my father is of an afternoon on holiday when I was six, when I took an endless walk, of maybe half a mile, along the beach with him on my own. Then we stopped at a café where he had a cup of tea and I had a drink of lemonade (in a bottle with a straw—what a treat!) which I made last as long as possible, in order to enjoy his exclusive attention for what felt like hours.

Available—to whom?

These days, constant availability can have its down side for our children. An answerphone is very useful at bedtimes—switching it on tells the child that they are our top priority and everyone else can wait. Conversely, let's be sure that mobile phones do not rob our children of the attention they deserve. Recent newspaper articles have shown the danger to families of workaholic parents who never leave the office behind and even take a mobile and a lap-top on holiday. I fear we are well on the way there: I visited Kew Gardens recently and observed a man speaking on his mobile, his young daughter by his side. He was totally ignoring the world-famous surroundings and also his companion, who can only have felt that the phone call was more important than their time together.

I returned to teaching part-time as our youngest child started school, and I was anxious to collect him at midday whenever possible in the two terms before he went to school full-time. So, four mornings a week, I rushed back from work to the infant school, hoping that the teacher would let them out a few minutes late. Then we'd ride home, with him still just small enough to sit in the child-seat on the back of the bike, and we'd collapse on the sofa together. We always had soup and a sandwich for lunch, because it was quick, filling and easy! I sometimes wondered if it was worth the rush—whether I should have asked someone else to collect him—but I knew the answer. We would never have that time again, and I wanted to make the most of it. My son once said to me, 'Mum, d'you remember when I was in Reception and we used to have soup for lunch, just the two of us…?' Enough said!

Personal space

One expression of each child's individuality is the need for their own space. This becomes more acute as they get older, and is very difficult for many families to provide. When children are under five, sharing a room does not often cause too many problems, although the older one's toys, models and treasured possessions may need to be put out of reach of their little brother or sister. I also think it is important to maintain the status quo and put younger children to bed first, allowing the older ones some privileges, even if this is complicated to achieve. I remember tucking one child up in bed while the next was having a story or watching a video downstairs and the oldest was getting out of the bath; I was fortunate that their father was usually home from work in time to be part of the balanc-ing act. But it is worth it: we can't expect older children to take responsibility later on—for example, with babysitting—if we don't treat them any differently from their younger siblings.

We have juggled every combination of sleeping arrangements, from three children in the same room to each on their own. The children's individual personalities have developed through having a space of their own, and then making the room 'work' for them… When separate rooms are totally impossible, it's still worth considering as many creative solutions as possible. One family of three boys did an annual swap-around so that every combination of 'two and one' was experienced, and each boy had a room of his own for one year in three. Interestingly, these brothers have very strong relationships with each other now, in their 20s. Another family built a half-wall to subdivide a large, long bedroom into two separate spaces, which worked well. However small the space, each child needs somewhere to call 'mine'. One of our children's rooms is roughly six feet square, but it's still enough to be 'a room of one's own'.

Sharing bedrooms with siblings is a common memory of many adults, usually reflecting on the problems caused. Often this stemmed from being forced to share with a sibling of the same sex, especially if another sibling of the opposite sex had the luxury of a single room. Also, as children get older, their different personalities often clash over tidiness, colour schemes, music, and anything else you can think of.

When children are given their own space, and not forced together, they tend to get on much better and choose to spend time together. Our daughters now choose to 'double up' whenever the opportunity arises, and love sharing a tent on holiday. Their brother also sneaks into their rooms (or tent) for a chat, a game of cards, or a midnight feast—to which their parents turn a blind eye, of course. On Christmas morning, they always open their stockings together, on the top bunk in the oldest's bedroom. I suspect they may still be doing this for many years yet, as long as Santa continues to visit.

Balancing act

The complexity of relationships within a family cannot be overstated. As parents, we need constantly to find the balance between focusing on individuals and on the whole family unit. One parent commented, 'We have always tried to recognize their own strengths and weaknesses, whilst, at the same time, being aware and alert to the needs of others, and to recognize the value of different responses.'

When this tricky balance is achieved, however temporarily, the family will become a dynamic and nurturing community for each of its members. In families where siblings relate well, there is less tension and competition, and the family is more outward-looking, able to include and support others. The fruits of this will be enjoyed for years to come by an ever-increasing family circle.

To order a copy of this book, please turn to page 157.

Recommended reading

Listening to People of Other Faiths

by Claire Disbrey

The world has changed. Once it seemed easy to say that only Christians knew the truth about God, and that they should go and share this truth with the 'lost', who tended to live in far-flung parts of the globe. These days, however, many of us find ourselves as neighbours and work colleagues of people who are sincerely committed to other faiths, and may have converted to those faiths from a nominal Christianity.

Respect for people's beliefs is essential, particularly in a culturally diverse society, but does that mean that we have to embrace the idea that all religions are basically saying the same thing or leading us by different routes to the same God? How do Christians reconcile this situation with their longing—and Jesus' command in the New Testament—to share our faith with others?

Listening to People of Other Faiths offers the chance simply to listen to ordinary people, who follow other faiths, talking about their experience of God, prayer, worship and ethical living. It provides a unique opportunity to hear before speaking, and to avoid making assumptions about how other faiths work in people's lives. Such assumptions can lead well-meaning Christians to answer questions that no one is asking.

The author, Dr Claire Disbrey, has structured the book with great care and clarity. There are three main sections—'Why we need to listen to people of other faiths', 'Listening to people of other faiths', and 'Talking about Jesus in today's world'. The middle section presents interviews with followers of the six main world religions—Hindus, Jews, Buddhists, Christians, Muslims and Sikhs. These interviews form a highly readable section at the centre of the book. Claire Disbrey paints lively word pictures not only of the people she meets but also the places where she meets them, from the interfaith representative at the recently built Hindu temple in Neasden, north London, to a Muslim woman based at the Central Mosque and

Islamic Cultural Centre in Regent's Park. She presents a transcription of her interviewee's words, with her own questions interspersed, but at the same time refrains from excessive comment and interpretation. This has the effect of allowing the reader to feel that they are genuinely listening in on the conversation, enabling them to start forming their own conclusions, rather than being told how, as Christians, they should respond to the statements made.

Some of the interviewees are British converts to the faith in question, such as Radha Mohan (born Richard Cole) who is a member of the Hare Krishna movement, and Estelle Rose who was born Jewish, married a Hindu and then became a Buddhist. We also hear from people who follow a faith that has been a feature of their family for many years, such as Brother Angelo, a Franciscan friar who grew up as a Christian, and Harkesh Kapoor, who spent his childhood as a Sikh in India.

Each of the interview chapters finishes with a sub-section headed 'Some Reflections', which highlights key aspects of the various encounters, by way of 'food for further thought'. This encouragement to thoughtful reflection is central to the book—in contrast to the kind of publications that focus on 'why Christians are completely right and all the others completely wrong'.

The opening chapters, meanwhile, present an overview of the place of religion in general in today's rapidly changing world, highlighting the challenges presented by trends such as increased secularization, globalization, and plurality (the multiplication of alternative worldviews). In response, religions can fall into one of two traps—changing too little or changing too much in an effort to have continuing relevance to society.

Perhaps the most challenging part of this book are the final three chapters, which reflect on conclusions drawn from the interviews to find ways forward for sensitive sharing of the Christian faith today. The author freely admits that she does not have all the answers but offers thoughts on ways forward in balancing the 'go and tell' command of the Gospels with the need to dialogue and form ongoing relationships with those who hold very different religious views from our own.

In writing this enlightening and thought-provoking book, Claire Disbrey draws on her experience as an Associate Lecturer for the Open University, teaching Religious Studies to undergraduates.

To order a copy of this book, please turn to page 157.

For reflection

The Pilgrim's Progress

by John Bunyan

Now I saw in my dream, that… the pilgrims were… entering into the country of Beulah… In this country the sun shineth night and day: wherefore this was beyond the Valley of the Shadow of Death, and also out of the reach of Giant Despair; neither could they from this place so much as see Doubting Castle. Here they were within sight of the city they were going to; also here met them some of the inhabitants thereof; for in this land the shining ones commonly walked, because it was upon the borders of heaven…

I saw, that as they went on, there met them two men in raiment that shone like gold… Christian then and his companion asked the men to go along with them: so they told them that they would… they went on together till they came in sight of the gate.

Now I further saw, that betwixt them and the gate was a river; but there was no bridge to go over, and the river was very deep. At the sight, therefore, of this river the pilgrims were much stunned; but the men that went with them said, You must go through, or you cannot come at the gate…

Then they addressed themselves to the water, and entering, Christian began to sink, and crying out to his good friend Hopeful, he said, I sink in deep waters; the billows go over my head… Then said the other, Be of good cheer, my brother: I feel the bottom, and it is good. Then said Christian, Ah! my friend, the sorrows of death have compassed me about, I shall not see the land that flows with milk and honey. And with that a great darkness and horror fell upon Christian, so that he could not see before him…

Hopeful therefore here had much ado to keep his brother's head above water… [and] did also endeavour to comfort him, saying, Brother, I see the gate, and men standing by to receive us; but Christian would answer, It is you, it is you they wait for; for you have been hopeful ever since I knew you… Then said Hopeful… These troubles and distresses that you go through in these waters, are no sign that God hath forsaken you; but are sent to try you, whether you will call to mind that which heretofore you have received of his goodness... Be of good cheer, Jesus Christ maketh thee whole.

And with that Christian brake out with a loud voice, Oh, I see him again; and he tells me, 'When thou passest through the waters, I will be with thee'... Then they both took courage... Christian, therefore, presently found ground to stand upon, and so it followed that the rest of the river was but shallow. Thus they got over.

Now, upon the bank of the river, on the other side, they saw the two shining men again, who there waited for them... saying, We are ministering spirits, sent forth to minister for those that shall be the heirs of salvation. Thus they went along towards the gate.

Now you must note, that the city stood upon a mighty hill; but the pilgrims went up that hill with ease, because they had these two men to lead them... They therefore went up here with much agility and speed, though the foundation upon which the city was framed was higher than the clouds... sweetly talking as they went, being comforted because they safely got over the river, and had such glorious companions to attend them.

The talk that they had with the shining ones was about the glory of the place... You are going now, said they, to the paradise of God, wherein you shall see the tree of life, and eat of the never-fading fruits thereof: and when you come there you shall have white robes given you, and your walk and talk shall be every day with the King, even all the days of eternity... There you shall not see again such things as you saw when you were in the lower region upon earth; to wit, sorrow, sickness, affliction, and death; 'For the former things are passed away.' ...

The men then asked, What must we do in the holy place? To whom it was answered, You must there receive the comfort of all your toil, and have joy for all your sorrow... In that place you must wear crowns of gold, and enjoy the perpetual sight and vision of the Holy One... There also you shall serve him continually with praise, with shouting and thanksgiving... There your eyes shall be delighted with seeing, and your ears with hearing the pleasant voice of the Mighty One. There you shall enjoy your friends again that are gone thither before you; and there you shall with joy receive even every one that follows into the holy place after you.

Taken from *The Pilgrim's Progress* (The Tenth Stage) by John Bunyan (1628–88)

Other Christina Press titles

Who'd Plant a Church? Diana Archer
£5.99 in UK
Planting an Anglican church from scratch, with a team of four—two adults and two children—is an unusual adventure even in these days. Diana Archer is a vicar's wife who gives a distinctive perspective on parish life.

Pathway Through Grief edited by Jean Watson
£6.99 in UK
Ten Christians, each bereaved, share their experience of loss. Frank and sensitive accounts offering comfort and reassurance to those recently bereaved. Jean Watson has lost her own husband and believes that those involved in counselling will also gain new insights from these honest personal chronicles.

God's Catalyst Rosemary Green
£8.99 in UK
Rosemary Green's international counselling ministry has prayer and listening to God at its heart. Changed lives and rekindled faith testify to God's healing power. Here she provides insight, inspiration and advice for both counsellors and concerned Christians who long to be channels of God's Spirit to help those in need. *God's Catalyst* is a unique tool for the non-specialist counsellor; for the pastor who has no training; for the Christian who wants to come alongside hurting friends.

Angels Keep Watch Carol Hathorne
£5.99 in UK
A true adventure showing how God still directs our lives,not with wind, earthquake or fire, but by the still, small voice.

'Go to Africa.' The Lord had been saying it for over forty years. At last, Carol Hathorne had obeyed, going out to Kenya with her husband. On the eastern side of Nairobi, where tourists never go, they came face to face with dangers, hardships and poverty on a daily basis, but experienced the joy of learning that Christianity is still growing in God's world.

Not a Super-Saint Liz Hansford
£6.99 in UK
'You might have thought Adrian Plass… had cornered the market in amusing diary writing. Well, check out Liz Hansford's often hilarious account of life as a Baptist minister's wife in Belfast. Highly recommended.' *The New Christian Herald*

Liz Hansford describes the outlandish situations which arise in the Manse, where life is both fraught and tremendous fun. *Not a Super-Saint* is for the ordinary Christian who feels they must be the only one who hasn't quite got it all together.

The Addiction of a Busy Life Edward England
£5.99 in UK
Twelve lessons from a devastating heart attack. Edward, a giant of Christian publishing in the UK, and founder of Christina Press, shares what the Lord taught him when his life nearly came to an abrupt end. Although not strictly a Christina title (Edward lacks the gender qualifications), we believe you may want to buy this for the busy men in your lives.

'A wonderful story of success and frailty, of love and suffering, of despair and hope. If you are too busy to read this book, you are too busy.' *Dr Michael Green*

Life Path Luci Shaw
£5.99 in UK
Personal and spiritual growth through journal writing. Life has a way of slipping out of the back door while we're not looking. Keeping a journal can enrich life as we live it, and bring it all back later. Luci Shaw shows how a journal can also help us grow in our walk with God.

Precious to God Sarah Bowen
£5.99 in UK
Two young people, delighted to be starting a family, have their expectations shattered by the arrival of a handicapped child. And yet this is only the first of many difficulties to be faced. What was initially a tragedy is, through faith, transformed into a story of inspiration, hope and spiritual enrichment.

All the above titles are available from Christian bookshops everywhere, or in case of difficulty, direct from Christina Press using the order form on page 156.

Other BRF titles

Seeking God's Face Beryl Adamsbaum
Learning to walk with God in prayer
£5.99 in UK

'I trust this little book will cause a yearning for God to rise up within you, a hunger and thirst for him that can only be assuaged as you come to him, feed on his Word, and seek his face in prayer.'

Writer, Bible study leader, teacher and speaker Beryl Adamsbaum helps us get in stride with God in the one essential, most powerful and dynamic relationship—prayer. In 14 short chapters, she encourages us to be grounded in scripture, to grow in confidence as we approach and communicate with God, to find sustenance for the times when God seems silent, and to walk with him into a deeper life of prayer.

The Lord's Prayer Unplugged Lucy Moore
A wealth of ideas opening up the prayer in ten sessions
£12.99 in UK

The Lord's Prayer Unplugged provides a unique opportunity to explore the biblical breadth and depth encapsulated in Jesus' famous prayer. The material can be used as a complete teaching programme over the course of ten weeks.

Alternatively, each unit stands alone so that the phrases can be studied separately and linked into the teaching of a Bible passage springing from the phrase. An index of Bible passages is included at the end of the book.

Each phrase of the prayer is explored through creative ideas, offering a wealth of thematic gems for teachers to pick and choose to suit their situation. Each unit includes:

Get your bearings
Why not decorate your space…
Quiet space
Icebreakers
Puppets
Bible exploring
Extra ideas
Prayer
Songs
Craft and art
Ongoing wall display

Easy Ways to Seasonal Fun for the Very Young Vicki Howie
Twelve Bible-based activities for 3–5s
£9.99 in UK

From January to December there is something for every season in this comprehensive teaching book for very young children.

Seasonal Fun for the Very Young provides the perfect complement to Vicki Howie's popular title, *Bible Fun for the Very Young*. Once again, Vicki offers twelve simple, off-the-peg sessions for those working with the 3–5s in primary education or church-based pre-school groups.

Each session uses strong visual aids for the single-focus teaching point, well within the experience of young children and appropriately introduced through Teddy and the story basket.

The twelve sessions give a wealth of ideas for every season of the year, including Advent, Christmas, Epiphany, Candlemas, Mothering Sunday, Palm Sunday, Easter, Pentecost, a teddy bears' picnic and a pram service for the summer, Harvest and All Saints' Day.

In the Palm of God's Hand Wendy Bray
A diary of living against the odds
£6.99 in UK

'Sharing a diary like this is about more than baring your soul. It's like taking your clothes off in public in mid-January and asking passers-by to throw snowballs at you. Not something you would do unless you hoped an awful lot of good would come of it. But here I am, doing it… Whatever good might result is God's to reveal. I would hope that it will involve glory to him and comfort and encouragement to others, as well as providing the occasional laugh.'

This prayer diary testifies how personal faith can transform the hardest of times, and how God's love and mercy still break through, no matter how tough the situation. Rob Parsons writes in the introduction: 'This is a book about trust. Not the kind of trust that says, "I know that soon it will be all right again", but rather the kind that trusts God—anyway—sometimes because there is just nowhere else to go.'

Winner: 'Biography of the Year', Christian Book Awards 2002

All the above titles are available from Christian bookshops everywhere or, in case of difficulty, direct from BRF using the order form on page 157.

Christina Press Publications Order Form

All of these publications are available from Christian bookshops everywhere or, in case of difficulty, direct from the publisher. Please make your selection below, complete the payment details and send your order with payment as appropriate to:

Christina Press Ltd, 17 Church Road, Tunbridge Wells, Kent TN1 1LG

		Qty	Price	Total
8700	God's Catalyst	____	£8.99	____
8702	Precious to God	____	£5.99	____
8703	Angels Keep Watch	____	£5.99	____
8704	Life Path	____	£5.99	____
8705	Pathway Through Grief	____	£6.99	____
8706	Who'd Plant a Church?	____	£5.99	____
8708	Not a Super-Saint	____	£6.99	____
8705	The Addiction of a Busy Life	____	£5.99	____

POSTAGE AND PACKING CHARGES				
	UK	Europe	Surface	Air Mail
£7.00 & under	£1.25	£2.25	£2.25	£3.50
£7.10–£29.99	£2.25	£5.50	£7.50	£11.00
£30.00 & over	free	prices on request		

Total cost of books £ ____
Postage and Packing £ ____
TOTAL £ ____

All prices are correct at time of going to press, are subject to the prevailing rate of VAT and may be subject to change without prior warning.

Name ________________________________

____

Address ________________________________

____

________________________________ Postcode ____________

Total enclosed £ ______ (cheques should be made payable to 'Christina Press Ltd')

☐ Please do not send me further information about Christina Press publications

DBDWG0304

BRF Publications Order Form

All of these publications are available from Christian bookshops everywhere, or in case of difficulty direct from the publisher. Please make your selection below, complete the payment details and send your order with payment as appropriate to:

BRF, First Floor, Elsfield Hall, 15–17 Elsfield Way, Oxford OX2 8FG

		Qty	Price	Total
184 3	Listening to People of Other Faiths	____	£7.99	____
260 2	Why Siblings Matter	____	£7.99	____
262 9	The Lord's Prayer Unplugged	____	£12.99	____
296 3	The Art of Waiting	____	£6.99	____
336 6	In the Palm of God's Hand	____	£6.99	____
342 0	Easy Ways to Seasonal Fun…	____	£9.99	____
370 6	Seeking God's Face	____	£5.99	____

POSTAGE AND PACKING CHARGES				
	UK	Europe	Surface	Air Mail
£7.00 & under	£1.25	£3.00	£3.50	£5.50
£7.10–£29.99	£2.25	£5.50	£6.50	£10.00
£30.00 & over	free	prices on request		

Total cost of books £ ____

Postage and Packing £ ____

TOTAL £ ____

All prices are correct at time of going to press, are subject to the prevailing rate of VAT and may be subject to change without prior warning.

Name ______________________________

Address ______________________________

____

____________________ Postcode __________

Total enclosed £ ______ (cheques should be made payable to 'BRF')

Payment by: cheque ❑ postal order ❑ Visa ❑ Mastercard ❑ Switch ❑

Card no. [ ][ ][ ][ ][ ][ ][ ][ ][ ][ ][ ][ ][ ][ ][ ][ ][ ][ ][ ]

Card expiry date [ ][ ][ ][ ] Issue number (Switch) [ ][ ][ ][ ]

Signature ______________________________

(essential if paying by credit/Switch card)

❑ Please do not send me further information about BRF publications

Visit the BRF website at www.brf.org.uk

DBDWG0304

BRF is a Registered Charity

Subscription Information

Each issue of *Day by Day with God* is available from Christian bookshops everywhere. Copies may also be available through your church Book Agent or from the person who distributes Bible reading notes in your church.

Alternatively you may obtain *Day by Day with God* on subscription direct from the publishers. There are two kinds of subscription:

Individual Subscriptions are for four copies or less, and include postage and packing. To order an annual Individual Subscription please complete the details on page 160 and send the coupon with payment to BRF in Oxford. You can also use the form to order a Gift Subscription for a friend.

Church Subscriptions are for five copies or more, sent to one address, and are supplied post free. Church Subscriptions run from 1 May to 30 April each year and are invoiced annually. To order a Church Subscription please complete the details opposite and send the coupon to BRF in Oxford. You will receive an invoice with the first issue of notes.

All subscription enquiries should be directed to:

BRF
First Floor
Elsfield Hall
15–17 Elsfield Way
Oxford
OX2 8FG

Tel: 01865 319700
Fax: 01865 319701
E-mail: subscriptions@brf.org.uk

Church Subscriptions

The Church Subscription rate for *Day by Day with God* will be £10.50 per person until April 2005.

❑ I would like to take out a church subscription for _____ (Qty) copies.

❑ Please start my order with the January / May / September 2005* issue.
I would like to pay annually/receive an invoice with each edition of the notes*.
(*Please delete as appropriate)

Please do not send any money with your order. Send your order to BRF and we will send you an invoice. The Church Subscription year is from May to April. If you start subscribing in the middle of a subscription year we will invoice you for the remaining number of issues left in that year.

Name and address of the person organising the Church Subscription:

Name ______________________________

Address ______________________________

____

____

Postcode ______________ Telephone ______________

Church ______________________________

Name of Minister ______________________________

Name and address of the person paying the invoice if the invoice needs to be sent directly to them:

Name ______________________________

Address ______________________________

____

Postcode ______________ Telephone ______________

Please send your coupon to:

BRF
First Floor
Elsfield Hall
15–17 Elsfield Way
Oxford
OX2 8FG

❑ Please do not send me further information about BRF publications

DBDWG0304 BRF is a Registered Charity

Individual Subscriptions

❑ I would like to give a gift subscription (please complete both name and address sections below)

❑ I would like to take out a subscription myself (complete name and address details only once)

The completed coupon should be sent with appropriate payment to BRF. Alternatively, please write to us quoting your name, address, the subscription you would like for either yourself or a friend (with their name and address), the start date and credit card number, expiry date and signature if paying by credit card.

Gift subscription name ______________________________
Gift subscription address ______________________________
____
______________________________ Postcode __________

Please send to the above for one year, beginning with the January / May / September 2005 issue: (delete as applicable)

	UK	Surface	Air Mail
Day by Day with God	❑ £12.45	❑ £13.80	❑ £16.05
2-year subscription	❑ £21.90	N/A	N/A

Please complete the payment details below and send your coupon, with appropriate payment, to BRF, First Floor, Elsfield Hall, 15–17 Elsfield Way, Oxford OX2 8FG

Your name ______________________________
Your address ______________________________
____
______________________________ Postcode __________

Total enclosed £ ______ (cheques should be made payable to 'BRF')
Payment by: cheque ❑ postal order ❑ Visa ❑ Mastercard ❑ Switch ❑

Card no. ☐☐☐☐☐☐☐☐☐☐☐☐☐☐☐☐☐☐☐

Card expiry date ☐☐☐☐ Issue number (Switch) ☐☐☐☐

Signature ______________________________
(essential if paying by credit/Switch card)

NB: These notes are also available from Christian bookshops everywhere.

❑ Please do not send me further information about BRF publications

DBDWG0304 BRF is a Registered Charity